# SCHOONER MASTER

A Portrait of David Stevens

# SCHOONER MASTER

A Portrait of David Stevens

Peter Carnahan

Chelsea Green Publishing Company
Chelsea, Vermont

Line drawings by Commander L.B. Jenson, C.D., originally published in *Atlantic Schooners,* copyright 1967 Atlantic Provinces Pavillion Expo '67

An excerpt from *Schooner Master: A portrait of David Stevens* first appeared in *The North American Review*

Excerpt from *Time Magazine,* copyright © 1972, by Time, Inc. All rights reserved. Reprinted by permission.

Library of Congress Cataloging-in-Publication Data

Carnahan, Peter M., 1931-
    Schooner master : a portrait of David Stevens / by Peter M.
Carnahan.
        p.    cm.
    ISBN 0-930031-23-7 (alk. paper) : $17.95
    1. Stevens, David, d. 1989.    2. Boatbuilders—Nova Scotia—
Biography.    3. Boatbuilding—Nova Scotia.    4. Schooners—Nova
Scotia.    I. Title.
VK140.5.S82C37    1989
623.8'223'092—dc20
    [B]                                                                89-32336
                                                                        CIP

# Contents

# Acknowledgments

My thanks go first and foremost to the subject of this book, David Stevens, a very private man who allowed me into his life and craft enough to write about them. I don't know whether David quite realized what he was agreeing to when he wrote a brief note in the spring of 1983, replying to my request to come up and dog his footsteps and write about him. But he proved to be a good sport and a deeply humorous man. He coped. So, too, did Evelyn Stevens, the other half of a remarkable fifty-nine-year partnership. Her warmth and care were constant factors in that household.

Dorothy Peill and Mary Dauphinee provided some of the most valuable insights into David and his work. Dorothy, in a long Sunday afternoon session peppered with her explosive humor, confirmed many of the points that I had tentatively arrived at after my first visit. She made me feel the book was possible. Mary Dauphinee, self-taught writer and painter, saw David through the eyes of an artist *as* an artist, a view that I came to adopt.

Thanks also to Murray Stevens, Harold Stevens and the many members of the Stevens families who talked with me and helped me. Their acceptance of a stranger in their midst was typical of the Nova Scotia character I try to record in this book: formal, genteel, cautious, understanding.

Many other Nova Scotians helped. Francine and Bart Shea offered both information and friendship in generous amounts. Kent Nason's film work added an indispensable element to the first section. I am grateful to Kent for the film and his other insights, and to Shelagh McKenzie, who arranged for me to view the film. Peter Brown, whose encyclopedic knowledge of Lunenburg and the South Shore was most helpful, originally introduced me to David Stevens. Rae Owen, of the Department of Tourism, introduced me to Nova Scotia and to Peter Brown. Alf Lohnes helped with technical questions about schooners, as did other members of the Nova Scotia Schooner Association.

Halifax and the South Shore are blessed with an unusual number of good writers, and their articles over the last fifteen years, carefully preserved by Evelyn Stevens in a family album, were an important source of research and verification. I have credited several writers in the text. In addition, I have used an occasional David Stevens quote when the reporter recorded a better phrase of David's or a more precise description than I found on my tapes or in my notes. Among those whose good ear helped in this way are Silver Donald Cameron, in his article "The Second Coming of the Schooner Comet," Peter Barss, and Linda Mason, whose many articles on David would make another book. Also, Silver Donald's book, *Schooner: Bluenose and Bluenose II*, helped me confirm my notes on those beautiful ships. The information on the *Sadie* and its owner, Hiram Tumblin, came from an article by Simon Watts in *Sailing Canada*, of which he is a contributing editor.

Among my American colleagues, I am particularly indebted to Pat Strachan for practical advice and encouragement, and to Robley Wilson, Jr., who gave a part of this book its first audience in *The North American Review*. Friends who helped were novelists Christopher Davis, Sharon Sheehe Stark, and David Small, poets Ed Ochester, Margot Barringer and Peter Oresick and non-fiction writer and mime (the written and the unspoken word) Dan Kamin. Stephen Berg, poet and magazine publisher, has my thanks for first suggesting this subject might make a book.

Closer to home, my cousin Charlie Stevens (no relation to David), a fanatic sailor and reader, checked the manuscript; my brother Michael loaned his library of sailing books. I am most grateful of all to my wife, Fran, for her support, her editorial skills and her patience. She is my first and best reader.

In one sense, this book is about a generation of people, my parents' generation, who lived in the twentieth century but did not lose the old skills of the hands. So in acknowledging help, I must acknowledge that generation: my mother, who was a weaver; my father, who couldn't stop fixing things around the house; their friends, Norman Archer, master of many trades; Bob Burt, who left the corporate life to build pine furniture. And a generation back, my grandfather, Dr. Frederick Malott, who taught me the proper use of the crosscut saw, a skill I shall never forget. When I met David Stevens I recognized in him the people who had brought me up.

Peter Carnahan<br>March 31, 1989

*For my generations*

# THE WOOD

$D$avid Stevens steps into the woodlot the way a man enters a room in his house, knowing where the furniture is without looking. The edge of the wood, beech and maple saplings and half-grown beech trees, rises straight as a wall against the grassy pasture we have walked through, past his small herd of twitching, fly-covered Guernseys; and stepping over the downed barbed wire and through the green wall into the interior is like entering a large, leafy house.

We are looking for stumps—stumps of the trees that made the keels of his last five boats; four schooners, one four times an international champion; another a replica of a boat his grandfather built in 1910; and a single sloop, made from the half-model that started Stevens in the boatbuilding business in 1945.

I ask about the woodlot and he explains the ownership. "The pasture was my brother Harold's land. When he sold it, I knew I'd have an awful mess—getting through another man's land to here. So I made an exchange for my plot down there."

"On the shore side."

"With the beautiful view, where the German's house is."

"When did you buy the woods?"

"1929. Well, I could look at the deed, but I'm pretty sure it was 1929. Good buy. Seemed a lot of money at the time, seven hundred and seventy dollars. Borrowed and scraped in order to have it. If I would've failed one year, the Old Captain would have been after me. . . ."

The Old Captain was his great-uncle, a retired sea captain, who took money out of the bank where it was earning 3 percent interest, and loaned it to his great-nephew at 5. "I paid him off, I think, in three years and he was quite disappointed. He said, 'I thought it would take you at least ten.' "

We walk a few steps into the wood. There are many small trunks but no underbrush; clusters of ferns make horizontal green planes a foot above the forest floor, a surface that parts as easily as shallow water as we walk. Dead branches spread on the ground like entanglements of old wire, the normal windfall of a wood; roots climb around and over boulders; lichens grey the north bark of the larger trees. The light on this half-cloudy day is indirect through the canopy of leaves. Glancing back, the light glares and throws the pasture out of focus, as if we were looking out through the sides of a tent.

Stevens stops by a stump with a large root system. It rises about a foot to a horizontal saw cut. The circle of wood, perhaps twenty inches in diameter, is yellow overlaid with a fine net of grey, the fibers along the edge burred and splintered by the force of the saw chain—a fairly recent cut.

"Here's where the keel and the stem and the stern was cut for the *Evelyn*."

"That's a good sized tree. That's oak?"

"White oak. Smooth bark."

The *Evelyn*, David Stevens' latest boat, will be a twenty-nine foot sloop, named for his wife of fifty-three years, who is at the moment back at the house cutting green beans and carrots for lunch. The hull of the *Evelyn* stands in the small, barn-roofed shop behind the house, resting on a keel of lead that weighs two thousand pounds, held in balance by six one-by-three struts, nailed from various parts of the hull up to the roof stringers. It seems to hang in the brown air above the shop floor. The hull is surrounded by a wooden scaffold supporting a walkway three feet off the floor to enable him to work on the upper planking and set in the final ribs.

Yesterday, while David Stevens was attending a meeting in Halifax to organize a welcome for the tall ships to Nova Scotia the following summer, I spent most of an hour in his shop, inspecting the hull of the *Evelyn* and the deep jumble of tools and scrap lumber that wash up to the four walls. By the doorway, metal-working tools—a grinder, two vises, hack saws, half-a-dozen blades for them, ball peen hammers—lie among scraps of pipe, cable, old propeller blades, tubes of caulking bent double and spilling their residue. One of the window panes above the bench is patched with a twelve-inch plank, rough cut from the mill, the bark still along one edge.

Along the north wall are woodworking tools: a circular saw, lathe and chisels, a heavy drill bit with a three-foot shank, draw knives, a hatchet, braces and bits, Robertson screwdrivers with the square post ends. The paint shop, at the far end of the bench, is as disreputable as any suburban householder's: drippy cans heavily encrusted around the lips; dead brushes, their bristles bent, tips stuck forever in coagulated goo.

The work benches are islands in a sea of lumber of every width and length, piled on the floor, completely covering a small woodstove, piled in racks along the wall at belt height, then at chest height, then overhead and, as the eye moves upward, piled finally on the roof stringers. Sawdust two inches deep covers the floor, and I stand in the middle of the shop inhaling the smell—dry, herbal, restorative—familiar to anyone who grew up with a tool bench in the basement or the garage or the back shed, transporting you instantly back to that child's moment when you first watched your father saw wood, watched the sawdust drain from the board and smelled the suddenly released fragrance of the cut. Some say wood will disappear as a building material within our children's lifetime. What a loss that would be. We sense it a bit every time we attempt the old atavistic gesture, "touch wood," in an automobile or a restaurant.

The wood in the floor-to-ceiling piles is mostly pine and rough-ripped oak planks with the bark on the edges, but here and there are patrician strips of mahogany, for while David Stevens will often plank a boat with pine he has cut from one of his own woodlots, the *Evelyn* has dramatically striped sides of light and dark mahogany, as smooth and elegant to the touch as a free-form table top.

As the hull stands amid the wash of used lumber and scaffolding, the striped planking emphasizes the lines of movement, curving down from the bow, swelling out in a pregnant curve at the widest point of beam, sweeping up in the most dramatic twist of wood, the seven-foot-long overhang of the stern. It is this final movement, extreme as the underside of a wave, that evokes, as the dry hull stands in the dusty and silent shop, the speed, the hiss, the whole ancient narrative of water moving along the hull — that passage that contains most of the design secrets of racing yachts.


"But how do you decide what *shape* it is?"

We are sitting in Stevens' dining room discussing a half-model that he holds in one hand. A half-model is a model of one-half a boat's hull, as if cut down the center line. If you put two half-models of the same boat together, port and starboard, you would be holding what looked like the hull of a child's model boat. Half-models are made to scale, usually one-half inch to the foot, and are used by David Stevens and other traditional boatbuilders instead of blueprints. Indeed, if given a set of plans, as Stevens has been on occasion by customers who know exactly what they want, he takes measurements off the plans and whittles a half-model. Then he reverses direction and draws his own plans on the traditional drafting board, literally a one-by-ten piece of plank on which the profile and sections of the hull are laid out to scale from the half-model.

I understand this perversity, watching Stevens sitting in his favorite corner at the end of a dun-colored sofa in his crowded dining room, running his fingers unconsciously along the curves of the half-model. For a traditional boatbuilder, much of the knowledge is in the hands.

"This is teak wood," he points to the top section of the model. "And this," the light-colored inlay that represents the waterline of the vessel, "is a piece of local pine. Below the waterline here is mahogany. You glue them together. Well, here. . . ." He takes up a rough block of three woods with crude saw cuts across two corners, indicating the possible beginning line of the curve from bow to stern. "Here's what we did last night. Robbie [his great-nephew, a blond young man in his early twenties who, like his cousins, refers to Stevens as "Granddaddy], Robbie wanted to make a model. So yesterday morning I glued the three pieces together. And last night ripped it out for him on the band saw. Well, maybe tonight he'll put her in the vise and start to work."

"And how does he decide on a hull configuration?"

"Well now, he didn't decide. I had the patterns—that's the pattern of the *Atlantica*, the one we built at Expo, a forty-seven-footer."

The *Atlantica* is Stevens' favorite boat but one. For Expo '67, Canada's centennial world's fair in Montreal, the sponsors of the Atlantic Provinces Pavilion, representing Nova Scotia, New Brunswick, Prince Edward Island and Newfoundland, commissioned Stevens to build a two-masted schooner to demonstrate the seafaring tradition of the Maritimes. Working under the flying canopy of the pavilion, Stevens and a crew of five workers set up the keel and ribs, and proceeded to build, rig, launch and sail the *Atlantica* during the six months of the fair. More than a million people watched her taking shape during the summer of 1967, probably the largest number ever to watch a boat under construction. One of the last visitors, that fall, was Queen Elizabeth II. A photograph of her greeting the ramrod figure of David Stevens is on the wall of the dining room where we are talking.

"I had the patterns for *Atlantica* right there in the shop and I just drew them off and sawed them out for Robbie."

"But he's got to do the finishing; he's got to really put the contours in."

"Oh yes, that's as far as I'm going with him."

"But he has a plan."

"Only in his head. I brought the original model out, and just left him look at it last night, only for a minute, and then I took it back again. I said, now I'm going to compare."

He puts the rough block back on the sofa cushion and picks up the teak-and-mahogany model. I return to the central question on my mind, "But when you make a boat, the shape of the hull is crucial. How do you decide that?"

He gives me a look as if I were being willfully slow, but his voice is patient. "Well, you have to have it so they break the water right, and leave it right." His fingers move along the curves of the hull.

"And how do you know that?"

"From experience, I guess. We had no test tanks. They have them down in New York, where they design these America's Cup defenders. And for all that, they still build three or four and take them out in the ocean and pick out the fastest one."

I try another tack, leaning over and pointing to the model in his hands. "If I were doing it, I wouldn't have so much bulge there—that would seem too much."

"Too sharp there? But you know a mackerel—a very fast-swimming fish—well their fullest point is right up forward. And then the tail runs out slim. All fast-swimming fish—the head part is the fullest, breaks the water—it's a lot easier to break the water than to drag it after you. And if you make a boat and she's too full here," he indicates the area past the midpoint, where the narrowing and rise to the stern begin, "or rounded too much, when she starts to sail she'll draw a wake up behind her, and that slows her up."

"Too full in the stern."

"Yep. And too short a turn up."

Standing at the stern of the *Evelyn*, I can lean my head against the bottom of the transom. The lines of the hull sweep down and out of sight around the broad beam of the center. I put my hand out to the extreme point of the curve under the transom, the point at which you feel the wood, in its violent reversal of direction, might explode. It recalls Paul Klee's dictum for architecture, "To stand, despite all possibility to fall."

I step back against a pile of lumber. From this angle the breadth of the beam narrows in an S-curve down to the four-inch oak keel, and the body of the boat suggests a wine glass supported on a fragile stem. I climb onto the scaffold and look down into the bowl of the empty hull, which seems at this moment in the half-light most like a vessel to hold air against the sea. Light slivers through the uncaulked seams. The narrow ribs, one every six inches, bend down in double curves to their notch points in the keel, as thin and strong as a line of dancers. I tap the top plank of the hull with my knuckles. There is a slight resonance.

The *Evelyn* will be an "S-boat," a marconi-rigged sloop built from the same half-model that started Stevens in the boat business thirty-eight years before. He picks the original S-boat model up from the sofa and holds it in his hands as he talks. "We'd been up to Halifax during the war, working for Silver's Agency repairing boats."

"What kind of boats?"

"Harbor craft. They were forty-six-foot, something like a Cape Island boat—used for ferrying servicemen back and forth to the ships. The ships were all up there in Bedford Basin, above the town. So we closed the farm here and I took my cattle right with me, to a farm near Dartmouth. A couple of cows, I think, and one or two calves with them. You know what they say, 'Two can live cheaper than one, and a cow is half the living.' And Doberman Pincers. We were raising Dobermans at the time. I think we repaired, in three years, between two and three hundred boats.

"It was pretty cold four, five months of the year. The work was out of doors, the cradles in amongst the ice, and you had to do a lot of that work bare-handed. But I got some experience — I probably worked on boats of every builder in Nova Scotia. *So*, we were there till forty-five and then we moved home. And then, of course, I had no money left. It took all that I could save up to pay for the trucks to bring us home. And I was obliged to go on unemployment insurance. Here I was, a turnip farmer on Second Peninsula, my fields lying idle for two years while we're up to Halifax. It was summer, nothing planted, nothing to harvest. Well, about that time, a group of six men from Lunenburg [his pronunciation makes it sound like Looneyburg], a couple of doctors, and the rest businessmen, approached me — could I build six day-sailers and have them ready for the season the next July? You see, there was no pleasuring during the war, and with the war over, they were anxious to get out on the water and sail."

"Had you been building boats before that?"

"No, I was a farmer. Oh, I'd built some, of course, and helped my dad and my grandfather. And we'd sailed for years at Chester, my dad and I."

"Why did they come to you?"

"I guess they figured I had some experience — part sailor and part builder — and they came to me and asked me to build a half-model. I got out my knife and whittled two of them, and then they came and picked out what they thought would be the best one."

"And you got the order."

"Well, there I was, no shop, no money, no electricity — and an order for six boats that had to be ready to sail in nine months."

"You weren't electrified then?"

"No, that came a couple of years after the war. So what I

did, I went down to Dad and he let me clear out some farm machinery from the sail loft, make enough space to lay the lines out on the floor—these are twenty-nine-foot boats, you know—and we built them right there on the plans, on the floor. I got a down payment of one-third, and I hired two of my cousins, Clarence and John Rhodenizer, and we went to work by the end of that month.

"Every plank was ripped by hand. The ceiling was so low in the sail loft we couldn't even put the cabins on—there was barely room to put in the ribs. But we started in and each one, when the hull was finished, we'd squeeze it around and out the door and line them up in the field outside. Well by March there were six hulls out there. Evelyn said they looked like they'd been put out to pasture. My dad made the sails, and my brother-in-law, he had the Dauphinee works, made the blocks. And on the twenty-fifth of June that next year, five days ahead of schedule, I remember, they all came over from Lunenburg—and six boats sailed out of the harbor." He sits back on the sofa, taking a pause. It is a story he has told often and, as in a well-staged monologue, there are moments for audience response.

"And you were in the boat business."

"Yes. Turnip farmer and boatbuilder."

"Why were they called S-boats?"

"That's just the name I picked for them."

"What does the S stand for?"

"Stevens. They cost eighteen hundred dollars each. And I hear one was sold just recently here for seven thousand dollars. Thirty-five years later. I actually didn't expect them to last any longer than thirty years at the most. And they're all six still going." He sits back again; and again the instinctive pause for response.

"Ah. And how many boats have you built since then?"

"My daughter asked me that a few years ago, and I said I didn't know, maybe fifty, and she said we should have a record of it—so she got a pencil and paper and I started reminiscing.

And we counted them up and I think it was sixty-four. Then I had forgotten two that came to me later, and since then, I've built three more."

The list, which Stevens' daughter, Dorothy Peill, later sent to me, runs to a page and a half of legal-size paper. It begins in 1921 with the entry "Motorboat for his father." After the boat business began in earnest in 1946 with "6 'S Class' yachts," there are as many motorboats as sailing boats for the next ten years, along with such pay-the-mortgage entries as "At least 6 flat bottom row boats."

In 1950 the first schooner appears, and then in the 1960s, schooners predominate, with the occasional ketch and a single bark (a hybrid of schooner and square rigging) in 1963, noted cryptically as "New Jersey." Many boats are identified with the owner's name, "Dr. Zuick, Miss Gillespie, Salter Innis, Capt. Angus Tanner, Mr. Kulukuntis (Greek shipping magnate)," others with often distant place names, "Baltimore, Nashua, N.H., Thunder Bay, New York, Lake Erie, California."

The entries after 1969 are less frequent. In that year Stevens turned the business over to his son Murray and retired— retirement meaning that he worked alone in his small shop across the driveway from his back door rather than with a crew. Under these conditions it took him three years to turn out his next boat, the forty-six-foot schooner *Kathi Anne II*. Since then he has built five more, his retirement fleet, one of them sold, the other four given to members of the family or kept and sailed. The final entry on the list is the *Evelyn*, still on the blocks in the shop, awaiting her deck beams, cabin and rigging. She is the first S-boat Stevens has built since 1947, and on the list she is boat number seventy.

The finger of land with the laconic name Second Peninsula extends four miles toward the Atlantic Ocean just north of the town of Lunenburg, a fishing and boatbuilding center an hour's drive from Halifax on Nova Scotia's South Shore. A mile from town a newly paved road leaves Route 3, the Lighthouse Route, at the head waters of long, thin Martin Cove, and winds in regular curves into bays, around headlands, down the peninsula. To the right is just the shoulder of the road and a line of small, round boulders that edge the water as neatly as a border in an English garden. To the left, high pastures and thick lots of black-green pines alternate, curving down to the road from the heights of the peninsula, a hundred feet above the water. The hills and the fertility of the fields and woodlots are unusual for Nova Scotia but characterize Lunenburg County, a garden patch on the glacier-scraped surface of the province, where the ice pack dropped an eon's collection of topsoil. Lunenburg County is famous for its cabbages and is one of the few places in Nova Scotia where farming competes with fishing as a reasonable means of livelihood.

The houses, one every quarter to third mile, are small, modernized, with well-kept house and barn yards. The neatness of the yards made a deep impression on David Stevens when, as a boy of twelve, he moved with his family from the barren, subsistence environment of Tancook Island. Second Peninsula, settled and cultivated by the same industrious German farmers who had founded Lunenburg in 1753, seemed to him a garden of lush order.

There are small, log docks on the water side of the road, with here and there a dorry, an aluminum outboard or a modest fiberglass cruiser at an orange buoy. Beyond Nichols Point, a single yacht is moored, a thirty-foot ketch with all its stainless steel equipment sparkling on its decks. Wildlife seems to coexist easily with the occasional passing car. An osprey, back-beating its wings to stand up in the air twenty feet above the water, prepares for a fishing dive. At low tide sandpipers skitter along the verge with their broken dot-dash runs, and a great blue heron can usually be found picking its way in the shallows.

The last third of the peninsula is Stevens country. Past the Second Peninsula School, now turned into a home with two front doors, the bay swings in deeply. Above it, as the land begins to rise, is a Cape Cod cottage set back against a stand of locust trees. This is the "old house" that belonged to one of Stevens' uncles. He recently has redone the interior in pine, and almost as an afterthought, built beds, cupboards, a buffet and other furniture. There is a yellow, freshly turned rim of earth in front of the house where he has dug a pond with his bulldozer. The road rises steeply, and at the hundred-foot level, set back between two stands of dense pines, is a modern, wood-and-glass house with top-of-the-world views northeast over Mahone Bay and southwest to the high ridge of the town of Lunenburg. David's son, Murray Stevens, built the house with his father's help in 1966, when he returned to Second Peninsula to join in the boat business. David Stevens' house, another hundred yards over the top of the hill, is the most modest on the road, a 1930s white bungalow, with that period's concave green roof curving down to squat, white pillars on the porch that runs across the front of the house. Ornamental cedars and other old plantings of the thirties, along with Evelyn Stevens' many hanging and standing flower pots, give the house the look of being sunk up to its shoulders in a garden.

Behind the house to the left is a cow barn, its red paint faded to a rakish pink, and directly to the left, thirty paces across the driveway circle from the back door of the house, what looks like a second, smaller barn, with the same faded green roof, red siding shingles and white trim. This building, however, has rows of six-over-six windows along three of its walls for working light; it is the shop where Stevens has built most of his seventy boats. From the shop door, one looks between the cow barn and the back of the house, down the hill to the brown sand curve of Backman's Bay and out across a five-mile stretch of water, usually punctuated with a few sails, to the low outline of Tancook Island.

Second Peninsula forms the western side of Mahone Bay, a major inlet of the Atlantic Ocean, nine miles wide across the mouth measured from the tip of the peninsula across Tancook Island to Blandford Head, and about the same distance deep to the spruce little town of Chester. The two settlements, Chester at the foot of the bay and Tancook guarding the mouth, are dramatically different in their appearance, history and economy and demonstrate the extremes of life along the South Shore.

Although on an island, the Tancook settlement is typical of hundreds of small villages that line the Nova Scotia coast where people take their living almost entirely from the sea. Each has its small harbor, usually with its concrete government wharf and a few brightly painted Cape Island boats tied up or at anchor in the water off a rocky beach.

Cape Island boats are the basic work and fishing boats of the coast. Still mostly built of wood, with a high bow for breasting the waves, a low, broad stern for ease in hauling fishing lines and nets, a small pilot house upright as a pulpit in between, they are the pickup trucks of the coastal towns, used for lobstering and for cod, haddock and mackerel fishing as far as the Ridge, twenty miles out in the Atlantic. This is the inshore fishing that can still be carried on by a man and his descendants with little more than family savings and an occasional mortgage. Offshore fishing, five hundred miles east-by-north on the Grand Banks, formerly carried on by squareriggers and schooners a hundred or more feet in length, is now the work of 150-ton trawlers, owned by corporations with boards of directors in Halifax and Montreal.

On the government wharf there is an equipment shack, and often a small processing shack — if the fish are cod they are still frequently salted before shipment — and behind them a stack or two of lobster pots, the arched grey cages that show up in so many tourist photos and watercolors. The houses of the town are placed at random along the stony rise of the shore, not following the street pattern, but each on its own plot turned so that the small, regular windows face the sea. (Even inland in Nova Scotia houses are placed up on the tops of rises and face the view.) They are mostly square boxes, the roofs steep, sides shingled, the doors and windows trimmed by a single, unmolded one-by-four. About half the houses are painted white, the rest garish shades of green, pink, salmon, purple or yellow, sometimes pink and green on the same house. The villages have the look of a scattering of child's blocks, colorful from a distance against a grey sea and sky, but up close, buttoned-up and bleak, despite the brave rainbow of colors.

I ask a number of city dwellers why the houses in the fishing towns are painted such vivid colors and receive no direct answer, embarrassed shrugs or sly comments like "Those are the Newfie houses." ("Newfies," for the residents of Newfoundland, are the country simpletons in the Canadian lexicon of ethnic humor — Polish jokes in the United States become Newfie jokes when they cross the border.) David Stevens gives me the first reasonable explanation for the color scheme: they paint their boats first, bright colors for recognition at sea, then the houses with what's left.

By contrast, the town of Chester is painted white, befitting its history of two widely separate influxes from New England. The first was in 1759, when the town was founded by settlers from the New England colonies. Nova Scotia is only a hundred miles across the water from the coast of Maine, although separated by more than six hundred miles of land that is still largely forest from the Canadian centers of Montreal and Ottawa. It has always turned its face toward New England, for commerce and to some extent for culture, and by the mid-eighteenth century frontier New Englanders, feeling crowded, were looking down east for more wilderness.

The older part of Chester, near the waterfront, is composed of clapboard houses on narrow, crooked lanes. Chestnuts shade the snug, fenced backyards, and heavy-leaved maples line the streets. Here or there a rambling rose dips over a white fence. One could be walking down a street in Kennebunkport or Gloucester.

The second American invasion began in the first decade of the twentieth century, when wealthy business and professional men brought their families and their servants to Chester for the summer. Those requiring more space than the quaint and crowded town could offer bought land on the peninsula that separates Chester harbor from the back harbor. Here there is a single, poorly paved road that feeds anonymous driveways. From the road the big houses are invisible among the trees. If you have a yacht – or a Cape Island boat – you can see them from the water.

Chester is a center for pleasure sailing, and as the warm weather begins, boats are launched, sails flown, forays begun into the 110 square miles of Mahone Bay and among its reputed 365 islands. It is a local saying that Mahone Bay has one island for every day of the year, but David Stevens disputes this – in a lifetime of sailing he has counted no more than a hundred. The season culminates in mid-August with Chester Race Week, when more than a hundred racing sloops sail triangular courses to the mouth of the bay, and past its two major islands, Big Tancook and Little Tancook, and their collections of white and colored fishermen's houses.


When David Stevens is asked, as he frequently is by newspaper and magazine writers, how he became a boatbuilder, he replies with a standard one-liner: "I was born on an island – the only means of escape was a boat."

The island is Big Tancook, where Stevens was born in 1907, the third child of Randolph Stevens, a sailmaker, boatbuilder, charter sailor, fisherman and farmer. The combination of jobs was typical of the times and is still typical of life in many parts of the Shore. Fishing and farming were warm weather activities. Survival during the cool months, the storm seasons when no sensible man would be out on the water, required other skills. "There was no unemployment insurance then." His grandfather, Amos Stevens, built fishing schooners and his father taught himself to make sails for them.

"Taught himself to make sails?" I am surprised, a bit skeptical at the lengthening list of talents of the Stevens family.

"Well, his father would build a boat and there were no sailmakers around at that time. He just took it up. You had to do everything you could in those days because you didn't have dollars enough. He could have came to Lunenburg, but that would have cost a lot of money, money that a Tancooker wouldn't have. So I guess he figured if anybody else could make a sail, so could he."

David's sister, Mary Dauphinee, a writer and artist who has taken on the task of chronicling the many branches and careers of the Stevens family, adds another piece of information. "He studied the curve of a gull's wing to get the pocket to catch and hold the wind. They were very creative men," she says admiringly.

"I remember one time," Stevens says, "he had a large sail to cut. And spread out, he didn't have a building big enough for that. So there was a pond there on Tancook and the ice was nice and smooth, and I went down on the pond and helped him to cut the sail. It was rather slippery, and we needed beach rocks to hold the canvas, but we picked out a very calm day and we did it. Cut on the ice. He was self-taught, but his sails turned out to be some of the best."

The sail business, which became R. B. Stevens and Company, Ltd., is still going strong under the direction of David's brother Harold, making four to five hundred suits of sails a year. Some are steadying sails for the local Cape Island boats, sails that help them keep bow to the wind so that all hands can haul nets, but most are sails for yachts throughout Canada and the United States. One of their recent jobs was a suit of sails for *Bluenose II*, the 143-foot schooner, flagship of Canada's sailing fleet, that was built in Lunenburg and returns there each winter for refitting. The *Bluenose II*, with its 129-foot and 154-foot masts, carries 11,690 square feet of sail.

By 1919 there were ten Stevens children to feed, clothe and care for, and during a particularly severe winter, survival on Tancook became difficult. Harold Stevens, eight years old at the time, remembers the family discussions during those winter nights.

"Mother had always absolutely refused to leave the island. She was born there and all her family were there. But there was no money. Dad couldn't rake scallops because the harbor was frozen. Finally he suggested he take one of the older boys and go to Halifax to find work. Mother said no, we'll move to the mainland."

That next summer Randolph Stevens bought farmland with a house and barn on a cleared hill that rises 150 feet above the water at the end of Second Peninsula. "Dad had to go into debt $2,900," David recounts, "to buy the farm, and the instruments, wagons and plows and so on—and he had to pay five percent interest." Without collateral, he could not go to the banks in Lunenburg. Here the Old Captain entered the picture for the first time, putting up his savings to help his relatives, and not incidentally, himself.

"To us, it was heaven on earth." Harold Stevens' eyes still lighten as he remembers as an eight-year-old discovering the fields and hills of Second Peninsula in midsummer. "Seventy-five, eighty acres—man! Young gaffers could run anywhere! Great life. Mother hated to leave her friends, of course, but once we got settled, she would never have gone back." He leans back in his chair—we are sitting in two kitchen chairs in the midst of the bare, varnished floor of the sail loft—and smiles again at the image in his head. "Great. I wouldn't give up the memory of those days for anything."

David Stevens was twelve years old at the time of the move, old enough to be aware that his father was adding farming to his two other principal occupations, sailmaking and captaining pleasure boats for the summer residents of Chester. David had finished the eighth grade at the school on Tancook, and in September of 1919, shortly after the family settled into their new house, he was enrolled in the one-room school a mile and a half down the peninsula toward town. "For two weeks every morning that September I would walk along the road past my father's fields, and I would just see all the work to be done. And when I got to school, studying didn't seem very important." He dropped out of school and told his father he would take over and run the farm. "In those days when you were twelve years old, you had to be a man—do a man's work."

"When Dad was in Chester for two months in the summer,"

Harold recalls, "David was more or less the captain of the family and the farm home. He was only thirteen, but somehow he was capable of ruling over us unruly young ones. He had that authority in him. Even his older brother, Amos, took the lead from him."

Dorothy Peill recalls the family stories of David at that age, "They say he got a beating every day of his life until the age of twelve. He just had so much energy, he would tease and torment the other children and have them in tears. Then when his father came home from Chester, they all told what he had done, and he was sent out to cut his own switch. But I've never heard him express any resentment about it. He knew he'd been a hellion." Dorothy Peill laughs easily and, when she is talking about her father, with great affection. Then she goes on more seriously, "After he took over the farm, my grandmother said he was never in any trouble. You always knew where David was after dinner—asleep on the couch."

The fact that he knew next to nothing about farming did not deter the twelve-year-old Stevens, as it has not deterred him in any of his later careers. "Such versatile men," Mary Dauphinee says of her brothers. "They don't run to town to get someone to do this and that. They do it themselves."

Young Stevens did have one piece of luck. "The man whose farm was across the road, Charley Berringer, his son had died the previous April, of appendicitis, I believe—well, I don't know if it was that or what, but he took me under his wing, taught me a great deal about farming. Without him, the first couple of years I might not have made it. I'd done a little weeding on the island, little things like that, and cabbage planting came natural to us—we'd seen that going on. We just planted them and put on lots of sea manure—eel grass and rock weed—and fishheads. One spring, my cousin and I sailed to Halifax five times for loads of fishheads. At two or three cents a pound for cabbage, we used to make a thousand dollars a year on that crop—and did everything by hand, except the plowing we did by ox team. But Charley Berringer—I learned many, many things from him. Raising cattle and handling an ox team. He and I used to travel together — we'd get up at two in the morning and take the loads of codfish into Lunenburg by ox team. The boats brought the fish in and we'd dry them on the shore and take them to market. I learned from him and I really liked him. He used to drink a little, but I must say, he never once offered me a drink. I always admired him for that."

During the next decade, with David handling the farm and his father the sailmaking business, they did well enough to pay off the Old Captain, and David, now twenty-two years old, took another loan from his great-uncle to buy the next piece of land, across the narrow, sandy isthmus that separated the Stevens property from the main part of the peninsula. At about the same time he met Evelyn Wight, a young woman from Port Medway, down the coast. By Dorothy's irreverent account: "She came down to visit relatives on the peninsula — and that cooked her goose. He had a lot of admirers, did Daddy, don't kid yourself. The women used to chase him, but he was a hard fish to catch."

Caught he was, however, and married a year later, in August 1930. The following summer, while he was working on a dredge in Lunenburg harbor, Stevens hired a crew of carpenters to build the small, white bungalow part way up the hill where he and Evelyn have lived since. His comments on the house typically have to do with wood and money. "My boss carpenter got twenty-seven cents an hour and he had two or three men with him, they got twenty-five. And the lumber, it was excellent good lumber, was delivered from a mill twelve miles from here by ox team, for sixteen dollars a thousand. Today for sixteen dollars you could pick that up and walk away with it."

By the beginning of World War II, David Stevens had been farming — raising cash crops of cabbage and turnips, with other vegetables, milk cows and beef cattle for family consumption — for twenty years. But in the manner of his father and grandfather, in the manner of other "poor Tancookers," he worked all along at a series of other jobs, most of them connected with the sea. While still a boy on Tancook, he decided against the most common occupation he saw around him, the marginal life of the small-boat fisherman, the life that appears picturesque in Winslow Homer paintings and television commercials but is primarily one of labor, occasional danger and, for the under-capitalized, poverty. A local saying goes, "A man who would go fishing for a living would go to Hell for a pastime."

"I did some lobster fishing and raked some scallops, but I didn't like the water well enough to make it my life's work. I was on to it enough to know what it was all about. I wasn't born for a fisherman."

While farming his new lands on Second Peninsula he worked for several years for Arthur Dauphinee, who had married his sister Mary. The Dauphinee block works, a very old business founded originally in the basement of a small building at the foot of Second Peninsula and moved later in the nineteenth century to a factory in Lunenburg, had manufactured wooden blocks, deadeyes and belaying pins for nearly a hundred years to equip sailing ships throughout the world. Blocks are the wooden shells that hold the pulleys used in a ship's rigging. Deadeyes, pierced round or teardrop-shaped pieces of wood, are used to tie off the shrouds, standing lines that do not move, while belaying pins are for the quick securing of moving lines. Taken together with rope, these three simple machines, all originally made of wood, are most of the tackle you need to rig a sailing vessel.

Talking with Mary Dauphinee in her home across the road from David's, I am taken into a small back room where rows of blocks are laid out to dry under a windowsill. "We bring them home to dip them in varnish," she explains. "It's a dust-free atmosphere and dipping avoids brush marks." Dauphinee blocks are made of *lignum vitae*, a close-grained, uncommonly durable wood from Jamaica that can withstand extremes of heat and cold. The blocks, about the size of human skulls, are a mysterious dark purple, the heart of the *lignum vitae*, some of them highlighted with stripes of light wood where the cut neared the surface of the trunk. Shining and exotic in the dim light from the window, they could as easily be rows of glazed ceramics set out from a kiln to cool.

Mary hands me a block she has picked from the row and smiles as my hand sinks under the unexpected weight. "They're very dense." Mary Dauphinee is a small, greying woman in a flowered blouse and sturdy denim skirt, with a quiet manner and the eye of a self-taught artist. Something—a look of receptiveness, the wisps of hair tailing off in different directions—reminds me of photographs of the poet Marianne Moore. Her watercolors of birds and her tapestry rugs hang on the walls of this room and the living and dining rooms. She looks at the glistening rows of shells for a moment and says, "They're the most durable and most beautiful marine utilities in the world." The block business, after 130 years serving the sailing trade, has nearly shut down. Competition from plastics and other materials is one reason. Another is the scarcity and rising cost of *lignum vitae*. The close-grained trees grow very slowly. "So slowly," she says, "they are almost not a renewable resource."

While he never actively took part in the sailmaking business built up by his father and carried on by his brothers Harold and Cecil, David Stevens did briefly emulate another brother, Spencer, who had established a successful mink farm. (Mink farming is a common off-season occupation in Nova Scotia fishing towns. Perhaps the most uncommon occupation was practiced by the fishermen of Cheticamp on the Cape Breton shore, who hooked rugs during the lean winters of the Depression.) By the late thirties, Spencer Stevens had developed one of the largest mink farms in the region, and David acquired 160 mink, but the experiment was short-lived. All 160 expired that summer of distemper. "I really wasn't cut out to be a mink farmer," he remarked.

Stevens was thirty-nine years old when he finally turned his hand to boatbuilding, but he had been a professional sailor, on and off between his farming chores, from the age of fourteen. In the first decade of the century his father ran day excursions for the new summer residents of Chester in his thirty-six-foot sloop, the *Mary S*, taking families for picnics out among the islands of Mahone Bay. The summer people soon bought their own yachts and hired Randolph Stevens and other local men to sail them.

"It was in 1908, I believe, he sailed a man by the name of Talcott. Went down to Bristol, Rhode Island, and brought up a New York thirty-footer for him in the spring, and sailed her here in the summer.

"They didn't sail their own boats?"

"They didn't know *how* to sail. And they were wealthy enough at that time they didn't have to handle their boats. Oh, occasionally when they would go out on picnics they would steer, but they wouldn't stoop to haul the sails.

"When I was aboard, it was racing — and Dad did the racing, because the competition was very keen. I hauled and trimmed sail, but in ten years with him I never got near the tiller.

"That was a boat called the *Dixie* we raced, about a forty-five-foot sloop. That began, I think, in 1919 — he sailed her for a lawyer from Baltimore, a Mr. Bartlett. And when Dad got too busy in the sail loft, then I sailed her for two or three summers. All in all, he sailed her for thirty-one summers, for the same family, thirty-one years."

Stevens does not mention that during that time, racing in Halifax harbor against the best sailors on the Atlantic coast, his father won the Prince of Wales Cup of the Royal Nova Scotia Yacht Squadron seven times. He does recount, however, with more than a little asperity, how his father's racing career ended. "They were winning too many races, my dad and the other local hired hands — they just became very good. So in 1930, the Chester Yacht Club made a rule that professionals could not take the tiller in a race. So from then on the owners had to sail their own boats."

"Did your father still go along?"

"He had to go along, yes. That was his job. And on picnic days he could take the tiller and sail as much as he liked. But on race days, he would trim the sheets and tell them which way to go, plot the strategy, you know, but the only time he was allowed to take the helm was to avoid an accident."

He leans back in the sofa and the tempo of his voice slows. "It was one of the hardest pills, I think, that Dad ever had to take — was to just sit there and not be able to take the tiller." He looks off across the room with his clear, helmsman's stare. "If there was one thing he loved, it was sailing a boat." It is not resentment in his voice but a certain coldness.

The sailing experience at Chester led to related jobs including, in 1932, the delivery of a forty-five-foot schooner to Montreal. It was the longest sail of his life up to that point and resulted in a peculiar experience for a sailor — he was shanghaied to captain a boat.

"I'd signed on as engineer just to get the boat to its buyer in Montreal, who would take it on to his place in Port Stanley on Lake Erie. Well, he met us in Montreal and he paid the crew off but wouldn't pay me. He said, You're not going home, I want you to run the engine for me as far as Port Stanley. Well, we argued for a while, but I didn't have enough money for a ticket home, so I had no choice. In other words, he shanghaied me. We started out, and up in the Thousand Islands we got struck by a line storm, worst storm I've ever been in. We almost lost the boat. And it scared him so, that night he came to me and said, I'm not going to allow you to go home at all. You have to stay with me until fall. So I did, and I went back the next two summers. It was Depression times and the money was good. We sailed over to Pennsylvania and Ohio and all up in Lake Superior, Harmony Harbor and Whitefish Bay. And by the end of three summers I'd paid off the Old Captain again, and so that was that."

In the late thirties, Stevens became sailing master at an American boys camp in Chester, but the camp closed with the outbreak of the war, and three years later he took his family to Halifax and signed on in the shipyards, beginning the work that would lead him in the end to the boatbuilding business.

"Most men around here can build a boat," Stevens says.

"We've grown up with it. I think it was the fact that I was a sailor, had been racing and sailing all those years, that made the difference. When I sit down to make a half-model," he says, offering that simple explanation, as ordinary and shifting as the surface of the water, "I just have a good idea of how it should be."

We have walked perhaps fifty yards into the woodlot and Stevens has identified three oaks large enough to make a keel for one of his schooners, with a fourth possible. He stands looking up a good-sized trunk toward the crown of dark leaves almost hidden by the lower layers of beech, ash and maple leaves. "Well, let's see now. I think I missed that fellow in looking around. That would make a keel for the *Kathi Anne* — if I wanted to make another one." We walk on, down a slight slope, stepping high to avoid the light grey boulders that litter the floor of the wood, and then stop to look around again through the filtered light that confuses my sense of depth, hitting some trunks, shadowing others.

David Stevens has the upright carriage of short-legged men, the carriage that suggests a military man, or the civilian equivalent, the captain of a square rigger. At seventy-six, the stance is slightly exaggerated, his front bowing out a bit, the legs planted a bit more firmly than the average seaman's, but there is no waste on the body, and the slightly bowed front seems more the result of a certain role he assumes — he likes to describe himself as an old character — than any fatigue of the frame. He moves with the stride of a man who walks all day and covers miles without seeming to hurry. His features are rectangular and strong, the face tanned but with relatively few lines for his age. In fact, his features seem to have squared up over the years, judging from photographs when he was in his forties and fifties. In one splendid picture in the family album of newspaper clippings, over the caption "Proud Boat-builders," Randolph Stevens sits with four of his sons and two grandsons before the stern of an unfinished yacht. Randolph wears a workman's cloth cap and stares off to the left of the camera with the solemnity found in nineteenth-century portraiture. The two ten-year-old grandsons stand behind, their hands formally on their fathers' shoulders. David's Murray, his shirt buttoned to the neck, his hair a pile of curls, stares as resolutely into the future as his grandfather. Robert, Harold's son, holds his face stiff but can't keep a smile from breaking his mouth. The four sons, seated down the row from their father, are less formal. Randolph Junior, who now works his father's farm at the end of the peninsula, folds his arms casually, waiting patiently for the shutter. Harold, the sailmaker, the only one with a mustache, gazes mildly ahead, looking as if he should have a pipe in his cupped hands. In the center of the frame, Cecil has turned and is looking down right, his expression unaccountably wistful. Next to his father, David Stevens gazes to the right of the lens with a full smile that draws his cheeks up in cheerful half-moons, the most ebullient figure in the group. The resemblance to the present David Stevens is apparent, especially in the winging eyebrows and the clear eyes that seem to attach to whatever they focus upon with the directness of a flashlight beam. But the face is fuller, rounder, more impish, with its lock of bushy hair in the middle of a receding forehead, its seemingly easy grin. In the years since the photograph was taken, the face has become leaner, the bones more prominent; the ebullience has become a bright, controlled flicker in the eyes. You have the feeling that all the irresolutions of a long life—the wrong turns, dead enthusiasms, lost ambitions—have been burned away, that you are down to the irreducible, the muscle, tendon and bone of the character. With artists who have achieved their pitch, the word for this is economy.

We walk on through the woods, Stevens ticking off a fifth oak with a wave of his hand, "That one will be ready in a year or two."

"What do you look for in a tree?"

"Well, soundness and straightness, and height without limbs." He turns right and walks into a cluster of saplings, putting his hand on a white trunk almost hidden by the congregation of grey-green beech leaves. "There's another pretty nice one. This is not quite as clean as that one. Got some limbs to clear off. Probably make a keel all right.

"Knots can be a problem. Sometimes they'll go in right to the heart. Spoils the whole tree." He sights up the trunk. "You could get a short keel out of him all right, a keel for the *Bonnie*."

The *Bonnie*, launched the previous summer, is the immediate predecessor of the *Evelyn*. When I first saw the *Bonnie*, on a snowy day in February the previous year, she was a hull set up on blocks in the shop, very much at the present stage of the *Evelyn*, and she seemed like a toy. She was just twenty-six feet overall, her lines taken off the hull of a work sloop called the *Sadie* that was rotting in a field on Bush Island. The *Sadie* had belonged to Hiram Tumblin, a fisherman who gained some notoriety as the local fishery warden, apprehending out-of-season lobstermen and other poachers. (His most-quoted line was an imperious "I seize those traps in the name of The Queen!") The *Sadie* had a long midsection for a sloop—Tumblin said she would carry twenty-five lobster traps, or a ton of fish when he sailed up the La Have River to the market wharf at Bridgewater to exchange them with the farm folk for vegetables, cheeses and home-knit mittens. Stevens took advantage of the extra length of the hull and added steps for two masts, turning her into a miniature schooner—thus her toy-like appearance.

Standing in the shop on that cold February morning of my first visit, I notice that the *Bonnie*'s sides are planked with white pine.

"It's all my own wood," Stevens says. "The keel and the ribs are oak from up the hill here, the planking from another lot I've got out near Maders Cove and the masts will be two black spruce from another lot."

"How many woodlots do you have?"

"A few. When it comes around to tax time, I get thirteen

different tax bills. I used to be in the lumber business, and I've held onto some."

Looking back on that talk, I wonder about Stevens' repeated characterization of himself as a "poor Tancooker." Friends tell a Stevens story that would seem to contradict this: that upon appearing at the bank one year to pay his thirteen tax bills, the teller remarked, "Mr. Stevens, you must be one of the richest men in Lunenburg."

David Stevens does not think of himself as a rich man. Not only does his life continue to be simple, labor-filled, devoid of luxuries, the tangible life of a dirt farmer, but that is his outlook as well. He sees the world and its people from the lower pasture, not from the paved highway. To him the residents of Lunenburg represent the rich, the privileged, those who have not really worked for a living, who made their money from rum running during the 1920s, a commerce that, as a lifetime teetotaler, he views with double disdain. And from some early epithet, forgotten by everyone but him, he sees himself reflected in their eyes as a "damn Tancooker," country-poor, an interloper.

His wealth, if such it is, is mainly in the unliquid form of forested land. When he began buying timber rights from landowners in the 1950s he found that, in many cases, they preferred to sell him the land cheaply rather than continue to pay taxes on land that was worthless for anything but the lumber. "They almost gave it away."

Much of the land Stevens bought had shore frontage, which became abruptly valuable as both Canadian and American speculators began buying up the Atlantic shore in the 1970s. Nova Scotians often remark on the fact, real or imagined, that the majority of their coastline is now owned by Americans. "Especially islands," Stevens says. "For a time there, people would do anything to get an island. They bought them up, and then they did nothing with them." Even today, most of the islands of Mahone Bay have no structures on them. "They weren't thinking about the inconvenience. These days people expect to drive up, to have everything right at their door." Islands used to be of even less value than woodlands. Stevens recalls that when he was buying his farm in 1929 it was found that two islands off the end of Second Peninsula, Goreham and Chockle Cap, were included in the deed. "We were sitting in Mr. Backman's outer office to sign the papers, and the clerk calls into the next room, 'Mr. Backman, what shall we do with these islands?' and he shouts back, 'Throw them in with the place!' "

I walk around the hull of the little *Bonnie*, standing on its keel in the shop.

"She's like a rowboat with masts. Why are you building a schooner so small?"

"I want a boat I can haul the sails myself," he replies, "So I don't have to get up a crew to go out for a day sail."

Logical, but if that were the only reason he could have built a sloop. I suspect for Stevens there is another challenge: to see just how small a schooner can be. He has already explored what is, for him, the other end of the scale. His largest schooners, the *Atlantica* and the *Margaret Anne*, are forty-seven feet. The reason for this upper limit has a typical Stevens logic. His shop is fifty feet long; he needs eighteen inches to get around the ends.


Stevens has found a large oak, the seventh he has identified as possible for "a keel for the *Kathi Anne*." He walks around to the back of it, sets his legs wide and reaches around the trunk with his arms, fingertips just touching on my side. "It's about six feet around."

We walk on through the wood, which fills now with a burst of yellow-green light. The sun has moved out fully for a moment from behind the long fingers of cloud that cover the peninsula, and the deep wood around us lights up with the suddenness of a stage set revealed behind a scrim. "Well, I'll tell you something. You'll have to see it to believe it, but I cut the keel for the *Kathi Anne* and for the *Comet* from the one stump."

"You mean from the same piece of wood?"

"Not from the same, from separate pieces. Two trunks out of the same root."

He quickens his pace slightly, peering into copses to the left and right as he walks. "The *Mora*'s in there," and a little farther on, gesturing to a large stump cut nearly level with the ground, "That's the *Margaret Anne*." I expect him to pause but he walks on determinedly, bending branches aside with both hands, letting them snap back without waiting for me to come up.

"There's one or two small ones there. Six or seven keels in all, I think, and some growing."

"That should hold you for a few years."

"Oh yeah, yeah. I'll never live long enough to use them up. There's keels here for Peter and Robbie." He stops and I come up to his shoulder to look at an old root system, grey and nearly clean of bark, a large stump cut close to the ground, the circle of the trunk discolored, nearly black with the weather, and from the same root, a second smaller stump that curves up to about three feet above the ground, where it has been lopped off by the chain saw.

"I'm pretty sure that's it." He studies the stump as if searching to recall a face. "I didn't think the stump was that high, but I guess it was. Anyway, that higher one made the *Comet*, and this one," he touches the rim of the circle with his boot, "made the keel for the *Kathi Anne*."

Of the sixty-nine boats that David Stevens has built, the *Kathi Anne II* is clearly the most important to him. References to her dot any conversation he carries on about sailing or boatbuilding. While she was the first boat he built in retirement, she is also *his* boat, the one he has kept for himself. Her sister ship, the *Margaret Anne*, was given to Murray for Christmas one year. The *Mora* was sold, and the *Comet*, based on a half-model from his grandfather Amos' boatshop, is designated for his grandchildren, so they can sail a boat designed almost a century ago by their great-great-grandfather.

It is the *Kathi Anne* that he continues to sail every summer, for pleasure and in the provincial and international races of the Nova Scotia Schooner Association. She is tied up now down at the anchorage behind the old homestead that Randolph Stevens bought for the family in 1919, her long, slim hull a bright turquoise, set off by a line of the copper paint that protects her hull from the waterline down to the lead of the keel. Her transom stern and two cabins are "bright," as they say locally, of natural, varnished wood. The fifty-two-foot mainmast, painted ocher, with a white topmast, is almost amidships; the forty-two-foot foremast at the front of the forward cabin. She is a spoonbow schooner, the stem piece of the bow curving down from the bowsprit into the water in a single motion, like the bowl of a spoon, as opposed to a clipperbow, in which the stem rises from the water into a reverse curve that reaches out along the bowsprit. A Nova Scotia naval ensign flies from the stern, eaten away by the wind so that the cross of Saint Andrew is off center. She is as sleek as any parvenu fiberglass craft, but without the stainless steel winches and turnbuckles that give those boats a glittering, mechanical look. Her natural wood cabins and light-colored rope and deadeye rigging give her a traditional air, a dowager of unyielding posture—dignified, dressed up in the middle of the day, not giving away anything to the younger generation. "She handles," he says admiringly. "I think of all I ever sailed, I think she responds to me better than any of them."

In the manner of proud men, those who make sure to have their own destinies in hand, Stevens appears to have forced himself into retirement. The six months spent in Montreal building the *Atlantica* at Expo '67 were the achievement of his life up to that time, the most demanding and the most heralded work he had done, and he returned to Second Peninsula that November exhausted, probably more mentally than physically. At the same time, he found himself unable to slow down. "I couldn't get a day off," said the man who had worked for himself for forty years. "There were boats to haul for the winter, a new contract for a ketch."

He plunged back into a round of building at age sixty that would have stopped a younger man. And not satisfied with working on the thirty-eight-foot ketch commissioned by a Dr. Duffy from New York, he began building a twenty-six-foot sloop, the *Hilda*, for himself. With characteristic scrupulousness he built on his own time. "I built her Saturdays and in the evenings. I had a fellow working with me and he lived with us during the week, and we'd go up to the shop after work, after supper, and work an hour or two." After a year and a half of this schedule there came a moment when the strain showed.

This is Stevens' version, repeated often now that the story has a satisfactory ending: "We were building a schooner called *Atlantis*. I was working on a slide for the main hatch, a piece of teak, and there were a couple of fellows working up on top, on the deck. Well, I passed the slide up to them, and a moment later I heard one of them say, in a low voice, you know, 'Look at this. The old man can't see any more.' I suppose," he says with an edge to his voice that is as close as he comes to irony, "it wasn't sanded just to their satisfaction. And the other said, 'Yes, he's failing pretty fast.' Well I guess that stung me — the idea that I was getting beyond it. And when that schooner sailed away in June, I went to Murray and said 'Do you want the business?' and he said he did, and I said, 'Well, it's yours.' "

Sixty-two years old, Stevens had talked himself out of a job. "That remark really put a burr under his saddle," Dorothy says. "He wandered around that summer and took it easy and he built a few little things, and then the fall came and he used to walk up to the shop and it was empty. And he didn't think at that point that he would build again, because he had really started to believe that he had passed the point, that he was finished. He figured, Maybe I'm not smart enough to see it, but everyone else is."

Building "a few little things" that summer included completing the *Pocahontas*, a thirty-four-foot Cape Island boat that the family still uses for utility work. "And then I played around a bit," Stevens says, "loafed around. When October came . . . I was . . . restless. I was feeling that I should be to work."

Upon accepting the business from his father, Murray had set about building a large new shop down the hill from David's house, on the edge of Backman's Bay. This left the old boat-shop beyond the Stevens back door empty and silent, suddenly as unemployed as the owner himself.

Standing in the doorway, looking at the strangely unclut-tered space where he had conceived and built forty-six boats, Stevens could tell himself that he was retired from boatbuild-ing, but for a man who had taken up his tools in that space for twenty-two years, it was not that easy to stop. For the artist, past achievements mean little; there is always something more to essay, a more vivid painting to be made, a more exotic sound to be coaxed from some new combination of instru-ments, a swifter and more natural boat to be built. And for the celebrant of the work ethic there is no question of stopping. (We drive through a field on the way to his sister Mary's house and he points to the ten thousand Norway spruce seedlings he planted two years before. To my casual remark, "You certainly keep busy," he gives the classic puritan response, "If I hadn't done something useful in a day, I shouldn't be allowed to sleep at night.") Looking around for an activity to keep himself alive, Stevens found his hands speculating again with wood — "I just got a couple pieces of wood glued together." He took out his knife and made a half-model for a forty-six-foot, two-masted schooner. He had his shop, a half-model, two thou-sand dollars in the bank, time and himself. In whatever word-less way, the *Kathi Anne* had already taken shape in his head.

He had never built a major boat by himself. Boatbuilding in Nova Scotia is not a solitary activity; it is communal, in many cases virtually a family affair. Randolph Stevens and his broth-ers assisted their father, Amos, in his boatyard on Tancook. David in his turn assisted his father, or when he himself want-ed to build a boat in the early years, his father made the half-model and then the sails. For his first professional commission, the six S-boats, it was two cousins he hired, and cousins — first, second, once or twice removed — of the numerous Stevens and Rhodenizer families had worked on his crews throughout the years of boatbuilding. But for the artist, the person driven by the goad of perfection, working with anyone, even a close family member, can be galling. Most creative arts are solitary activities, so the person wrestling with his personal vision and his personal standards does not injure those close by. When the arts must be communal, they are famous for dischord, displays of "artistic temperament."

Stevens spoke briefly and bitterly of his crew in Montreal, a larger group than he normally worked with, extending farther out from the family. One member at least — he doesn't specify — objected to his driving leadership and began inciting the others to strike. One day at the pavilion they walked in as a group and presented their demands. Stevens, his attention focussed on the boat taking shape in his head, on the actual boat taking shape under the front canopy, watched by tens of thousands of visitors each day, on the carefully calculated daily rhythms that would bring them, with no time to spare, up to the moment of launch in mid-October, found this development appalling and wounding. It is an injury against which there is no defense. The severity of the age-old penalty for mutiny probably springs from this — the distractedness, and thus the vulnerability of command. To the leader, the experience is not just threatening to his physical world and plans, it is an attack on his spiritual progress — he is advancing on his City on the Hill, only to be brought up by the footsore, who didn't think to wear the proper shoes. Stevens eventually worked out a compromise with his crew that resulted in the most disgruntled member returning to Lunenburg and the work continuing with the others, but it is clear from the tone of his voice years later sitting in his dining room that he still finds the incident deeply dispiriting.

Advancing age does not increase the tolerance. Things seem to have built up for Stevens — the Montreal confrontation, the "old man" remark from his family crew, perhaps too the sense of finiteness with which a person passing the age of sixty begins to count the years remaining. It is easy to imagine a state of mind common in older people: after a lifetime of accommodation and compromise, you realize you have limited time left; you go your own way. By contrast to the middle years, when time is spent, often lavishly spent, talking other people around, listening, being diplomatic (a member of the selection committee for Expo: "We had to have a diplomat—this is where Stevens excelled."), at sixty, or at some point where you begin to live with your mortality, there can be a feeling of *no more*—there it is; take it or leave it. Timon retires to his cave; Tolstoy sets out on a journey. You see what you have to do and you have no time for the opinion of others. To a good extent the Stevenses had always lived in this direct way, seen what they had to do, gone and done it. No time, no money, as they often say, to bring someone from Lunenburg. In a subsistence world it was practical, and practice becomes pride. The idea of building a schooner by himself, with wood from his own land, must have seemed to David Stevens both a natural and a saving grace. In age, as in youth, independence has to be won again and again.

The building began with two old bathtubs and a pile of used automobile and truck tires. The bathtubs he suspended between two I-beams set in the tall grass behind his shop, the tires were stacked under and around them and doused with fuel oil. Chunks of lead went into the tubs and the whole mass was set alight. When the lead had melted it was ladled out and carried to the shop, and there poured into a long, masonite-lined trough, a mold for the lead keel, a sixty-eight-hundred-pound bottom piece bolted to the oak keel, providing the ballast for the schooner. A lead keel is a relatively new technique in Nova Scotia, referred to as "outside ballast." In the days of Stevens' grandfather, Amos, "inside ballast" was more often the rule, consisting of good-sized beach rocks laid in the bottom of the hull between the ribs. Inside ballast could shift, of course, but it had one advantage over the lead keel: if the boat ran aground you could throw rocks overboard until she floated.

Although he had in mind to build the *Kathi Anne* with his own wood, for the oak keel, the longest and largest member in the hull to which all other structural pieces are attached, he went to two of the lumber yards that he usually dealt with. "I was disappointed right at the very start," he says. "I couldn't find a piece of oak large enough. It had to be twenty-four feet in a piece. Well, I came back here to this lot and I found this stump. You see here." He squats down and points to the pattern of earth around the dual stump. "This is actually an old stump that someone cut years ago, before I had the land. And these two shoots grew out of it. And I looked at them and I said to the biggest one, 'You'll make it.' I went home and got the old tractor and a power saw and came back. This one had quite a bend into it; I had to cut four feet off. But I cut him down and hauled him home, outside the shop. I got Randy's trailer and I loaded him alone."

"A twenty-four-foot trunk?"

"Yeah, all alone."

On a previous day I had watched Stevens work with a pee-vee, a lumberman's metal-tipped pike with a curved, hinged claw on one side, moving and sorting a pile of cut timbers. Some were a foot wide and as much as eighteen feet long, but my offer of assistance was refused. He worked steadily, putting some on the pile for firewood, others in the pile for boat lumber, loading a few on a trailer to be taken down to the anchorage, moving the pieces as easily as I would have moved two-by-fours, demonstrating in this matter-of-fact ballet his years of working alone, his by now nearly unconscious sense of levers and fulcrums, using the other pieces, the ground, gravity, as if they were another person.

"So I loaded it, took it to the mill out here about ten miles at Northwest, had it sawed and brought home, and by five o'clock that evening it was sitting on the blocks in the shop, all ready to go."

He straightens up and gives a short nod of his head, "I'm not beat yet!" His voice carries the peculiar resonance of defiance mixed with pleasure, as he acts out again the moment, standing over the roughed-out keel in the old shop, when he felt himself launched on a new and solitary career.

"I'm not beat yet!"


Laying down the lines is the most mysterious, certainly the most complex, part of the boatbuilder's art. In most boatshops it is done from plans that are daunting to a layman. The detailed drawings of the marine architect fan out across the page in cages of parabolic lines, as abstract as music, laying out for the builder in a web of calculus every theoretical moment on every curve of the boat's hull. For builders like Stevens the process is equally mysterious but simpler in execution. After I had puzzled over the maze of lines, steps and formulae in half-a-dozen books on wooden boat construction, I asked Stevens to explain to me how he turned his plan into the hull of a boat.

"Well of course the half-model comes first." He holds up the teak and mahogany model we have been talking about in his dining room. "And then we draft her off. I've got a drafting board upstairs somewhere."

He leaves the room and I hear him clambering up the narrow stairs to the upper floor. He returns with a one-by-ten piece of pine board about two feet long. The outline of a half-model has been traced on it. To illustrate he takes the half-

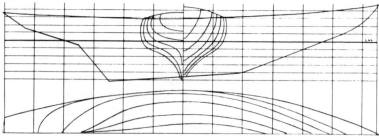

Lines taken from a half model.

model from the sofa and slaps it with a dry clack against the profile on the board. I nod to show that I understand at least that much. The hull profile on the board is divided into sections by a grid of regular horizontal and vertical lines. To the left of each vertical a curved line bends down to the bottom of the profile. The curved lines are slim at the bow, belly out into S-curves at points amidships and narrow again toward the stern. It is clear they are sections, as if the hull were sliced through at various points from stem to stern. Looking at them I begin to see the shape of the boat transferred into two dimensions. "How do you get those curved lines?"

"From the model. I just take a thin piece of pine, very soft, very easy to work, and I chip it out until it fits right in here on the model." With his finger, he traces the curve from the sheer line of the model vertically down to the keel. The piece of white pine would fit snugly against the side of the model, reflecting the curve exactly.

"So you just whittle a piece of pine and fit it in there on the side of the model?"

"One at each of these points. Very easy—takes about an hour, two hours I guess to do a half-model like this one. Then I take the pieces of pine, lay them on the drafting board and trace them off."

"And that gives you those curved lines?"

"Yes, the lines of the hull. You could take a piece of sheet lead and bend it and scribe it. Anything that would give you the shape."

"But that's simple!"

"Of course it's simple," he says with a touch of impatience. "Well good grief, years ago a lot of the people who built these boats couldn't read or write. I remember my grandfather getting the newspaper on Tancook, sitting out in summer and reading the paper to some of the people. It wasn't that they were stupid or anything like that. They didn't have the chance to learn."

He pauses for a moment, as if I had led him away from the subject, and then picks up the pine board from the sofa. "So, that's the drafting board. Then we lay the lines down on the floor."

"You do what?"

"I lay the profile, this," he holds up the drafting board again, "down on the shop floor."

"Full size?"

"Full size. That's what these measurements are here."

I inspect the drafting board more closely. It is filled with numbers. The curved sections are drawn at numbered verticals about every two inches from stem to stern. Other numbers, in feet and inches, have been inserted in each box made by the lines of the grid, giving the profile a whimsical cargo, as if it were a drawing by Saul Steinberg called "Ship of Numbers." The numbered verticals, Stevens explains, are the locations of the key ribs. Applying the half-inch-to-the-foot scale will give him ribs every four feet along the keel, enough to define roughly the shape of the hull. The boxed numbers, which progress from bottom to top — one foot one inch, one foot three inches, one foot six inches, and so forth — are the measurements from each vertical to its curved line. They define the curve of the rib as it is laid down full-sized on the floor.

"As I lay them down, I keep measuring and checking with the drafting board." Stevens explains that he doesn't actually draw the section lines on the floor (many boatbuilders do, or draw them on large sheets of paper laid on the floor), but rather moves to the floor of his boatshop at this point and puts down small wooden cleats at the key points of his diagram, to which he bends the actual ribs.

In whatever way the lines are marked on the floor, at this point most boatbuilders would use them to cut molds, full-sized pieces that would reflect the curves of the hull at particular points between stem and stern. A succession of these molds would be set up in the shop on either side of the keel, and the ribs that give the hull its shape bent to the molds. Stevens shortcuts the process by steaming the strips of white oak that will be the ribs and bending them right on the plan, on the shop floor. "Then I put battens on — scrap lumber that's lying

Drafting board and half model.

around — just tack them on to hold the shape when it cools."

The shaped ribs, held in place by the battens, are lifted off the floor and nailed directly into the keel of the boat at the four-foot intervals indicated on the drafting board. They are held upright from stem to stern by horizontal stringers, ribbands thin enough to flex around the curves of the wide parts of the hull. This is another point at which he checks the hull shape. "When you put these ribbands around, any little slack or high spots, you can always tell. So you're adjusting as you go." The ribbands will be removed, each in its turn, as the planking reaches it.

The skeleton of the boat is now revealed, standing upright in the shop, the full height of the hull showing for the first time. It suggests the finished boat to the extent that a structure of dinosaur bones in a museum suggests the living creature, a dramatic sketch but still abstract, full of air.

The use of a few key ribs to establish the shape of the hull could be disastrous for a novice builder, but Stevens needs only these points of reference to create, with the other ribs that are now steamed, bent and nailed in place, curves as smooth as any architect's fancy. It is one of the many parts of the process that are so instinctive by now, so much in his hands, that he has difficulty talking about them with his usual precision: "You don't have to make but a few. You get those right, and then you make it all even."

"And the others fall into place?"

"Yeah. It's very simple."

When Stevens made the decision to build the *Kathi Anne* by himself he was practical enough to ask for help at the points where it was essential. The first was the pouring of the sixty-eight-hundred-pound lead keel. The lead had to be ladled from the bathtubs behind the shop, where it was melted, carried in to the long masonite trough that was the mold, and poured. "You must have a continuous pour. With only one hand doing it, it could cool and you'd have a break and it'd be no good."

He enlisted Jim Rhodenizer, a nephew of the cousins who had been his construction crew on the original S-boats and one of his best workers during the later years of his boat business, to help pour the lead and help with the setting of the ribs and the beginning rows of planking. By this time, however, Murray had begun work on his first commissioned boat and part of the agreement between father and son was that the crew members would follow the business. So Jim Rhodenizer went down the hill to Murray's new boatshop and Stevens faced the problem of planking.

"I'll never forget, when the ribs were in, one of the men that worked with me for twenty years, he stood there and looked at it and he said, You know you can't plank this boat by yourself. I said, Is that so? No, he said, you can't. Well, I said, I'll show you."

Now he began his odyssey in earnest, working out the long-familiar actions of his boat-building crew in terms of a single man, two hands, one point of support. This time, to escape from his metaphorical island, he had to build the boat alone.


Kent Nason is a young filmmaker with the Atlantic Studios of the National Film Board of Canada. Between other assignments that take him as far afield as Indonesia and the People's

Republic of China, he drives down every month or two to Second Peninsula, forty minutes from his home in Hubbards, and shoots footage of Stevens putting together the *Evelyn*. It is a speculative venture; Nason is not yet to the point where he knows whether or not he has a film. But the rushes to date — a disjointed collection of establishing shots of the house, boat-shop, cows in a field, the curve of Backman's Bay, along with sound sequences of Stevens talking about boatbuilding while sitting in his shop, his hands sanding a piece of molding or moving along the contours of a half-model — make fascinating viewing. Most interesting of all is the silent footage, shot over a period of about eight months, of Stevens setting up the keel, the bow and stern pieces, setting in the ribs, and planking the *Evelyn*.

I sit in one of the Atlantic Studios editing rooms in Halifax and run these sequences over and over at the large console of the editing machine, forward first, then backward, then with

Nason arrived with his camera after the lead keel had been poured, so in his first shots the lead is already there, a one-ton bar standing free on the shop floor. The double doors at the back of the shop are open and the daylight reflects off the top and sides of the lead, a deep metalic blue where it is unmarked from the mold, bright silver where Stevens has planed it. As is, it could stand on a corporate lawn for a metal sculpture. We cut to a close shot of Stevens working on the top of the lead with a mallet and chisel, then to a shot of him planing the top of the lead with a wood plane, pushing up bright silver curls of lead through the slot above the blade. The wooden keel can be seen in the background, its regular rectangular notches for the ribs suggesting large dentil molding. Then Stevens is doing the same planing action on the wood keel, stopping occasionally to check the surface with an L-square. He planes in long, quick strokes with the easy, unhesitating rhythm of someone rowing a boat.

In the next shot, time has been excised and we are looking from a medium distance at the assembled keel and stem piece. The first two-and-a-half feet of the base is the dark blue lead, and the layer on top of that the blond wood of the keel. From the front of this heavy, rectangular body, the stem piece, also of the blond white oak, extends at a forty-five-degree angle upwards toward what will be the surface of the water and five feet beyond in a dramatic diagonal. The camera cuts in to the scarf, the overlapping joint where the keel joins the stem, and begins a slow pan up the stem piece, ending in the final, gentle turn up of the bow; then back for a long shot of the whole structure, its heavy body and arching neck reminding me, as much as anything, of a giraffe lying down, a two-dimensional giraffe, like a cut-out for a child's zoo.

The stern post is the final piece of the keel assembly, made from the last piece of the trunk cut in the oak lot up the hill. As thick as the keel and, on the *Evelyn*, about six feet long, it extends upward at fifty-five degrees from the end of the keel and will carry the rudder stock, a bronze rod connecting the rudder with the helmsman's wheel on deck. This is the first shot in which I can imagine other hands helping. Instead, Stevens has raised the heavy post on a chain pulley hung from the barn stringers and is guiding it, suspended at the right height, into the joint with the keel. The bolt hole has been

Stern, keel, and stern post in place.

drilled previously and, holding the post from swaying on its chain, he guides a long bronze bolt through and tightens a nut on top with a socket wrench, stopping periodically to check the plumb of the post with a level.

In a slightly tighter shot, I recognize the yolk-shaped piece that will make the transom, the flat stern plate of the hull, suspended on the chain as Stevens bolts it into place crossing the upper part of the stern post. At first I am distracted by what appears to be a thin yellow ribbon running horizontally across the camera frame, until, the transom in place, Stevens pulls the ribbon against its back edge and I see it is a tape measure, strung between the bow and some point at the back wall of the shop so that he can check the measurements without letting go of the transom while maneuvering it into place.

Setting the key ribs on the backbone of the keel is a heavy job and Stevens would ordinarily need help with this, but the *Evelyn* is a small enough boat that he apparently feels he can do it alone. In the next shot he walks into the camera frame and lifts from the floor, where it has been bent to shape on cleats, the first rib section, the first piece that will give breadth to the hull. It is essentially a U-shaped piece, the two ribs turning downward again at the bottom of the arc, separated by a four-inch space where they will fit into notches on either side of the keel. They are held in shape by a temporary bracing of scrap boards from around the shop, making an awkward structure about eight feet across that Stevens staggers with, his arms spread wide, as he lifts it above the keel. Wrestling it into the notches in the keel, he holds it upright with one arm, reaching down with the other to insert two nails in holes previously drilled in the end of each rib piece. A hammer appears from somewhere and he drives the nails into the keel. One nail bends over but he continues to pound the shaft into the surface of the wood—fastening is the point here; aesthetics can be dealt with later. He stands back from the precariously attached piece and for the first time we see the third dimension of the hull.

Here again there is a time break, for when we next see the

hull it is a complete skeleton. All the key ribs are in, held in place by the series of narrow, horizontal ribbands, bending around the girth of the hull from narrow bow to narrow stern. It is a cold winter day but the doors of the boatshop are wide open and against the grey mist outside we see the steambox, the size of a tall man's coffin, resting horizontally above four sixty-gallon steel drums, the boilers of the Rube Goldberg steam machine. Stevens is inside the bow of the *Evelyn*; his helper, a tall, heavy-set young man, red-cheeked in the cold, walks quickly outside, opens the end of the box, releasing a belch of steam, and comes back with a short piece of oak, its surface glistening with water drops and linseed oil. Stevens chips the end, wielding a drawknife like a hatchet, and insets the piece near the bow, bending it by hand to the curve defined by the ribbands. Moving quickly, the breath steaming from his mouth, the young man secures it temporarily with several nails through the ribbands.

Setting in the final ribs is a job for which Stevens always uses help. Given his other ingenious circumventions, it is possible that he could devise some way of bending the wood on the inside of the hull and nailing while he is bending it, but the

Ribbands around from bow to stern.

complicating factor here is time. The steamed pieces from the box only hold their heat, and their flexibility, for about ten minutes. Perhaps they would hold longer in warmer weather, but Stevens usually cuts his keels in autumn, when the sap is down in the wood, and the steaming of the ribs follows around midwinter. Then too, he is following an ancient pattern: boatbuilding is a winter activity, the other side of the year from fishing and farming. Even retired as he is, the summers, with their long light evenings and the house constantly alive with grandchildren on vacation, are given over to sailing, racing and family activities. Boatbuilding continues to be for the dark and more solitary winter days.

The next series of shots shows Stevens planking the hull, working about a third of the way up the side of the boat. He walks into the frame with the next board and begins fitting one end into the rabbet, the groove that accepts the ends of the planks so they make a flush surface with the stem piece. Before beginning this he slips the other end of the board into a looped cord that is hanging over the side of the boat. For a moment I don't understand what he is doing with this oddly dangling piece of cord. Then it becomes clear that the cord is the helper, replacing the other person who would hold the plank while he fitted the rabbet end.

When he is satisfied that the plank fits properly, a series of large wedges are driven in between the plank and the next ribband, again surrogates for hands to hold it in place for the drilling and nailing.

Nason's view of this next sequence is close up, showing just the rich mahogany side of the boat, the drill, Stevens' head and shoulder, his knitted wool cap and red plaid wool shirt indicating we are still in heavy winter. The countersink hole is drilled first, about a half inch across and a quarter inch deep. This sets the head of the nail below the surface, for protection from the water and also because, plugged with a wooden dowel of mahogany, it makes a beautiful finish. "Like furniture," is Stevens' description.

He drills an upper and lower hole at each rib freehand,

without measured marks, and moves on quickly to the next rib. The drill appears again with a smaller bit and bores the nail hole in the center of the first hole. The thin copper nail, glinting in the camera lights, is driven in, and a fourth pass is made with a punch to drive it through so the point protrudes on the inside of the rib. At this stage a helper would normally brace the nail on the outside while Stevens moves inside, slips a washer over the nail end, clips the end off and pounds it flat, creating a rivet.

This is one of the jobs for which he must have help, but Stevens does not want another man standing around day after day while he cuts, fits, drills and nails each plank, so he has come up with one more ingenious solo technique: "I bore the holes so small that you can just get the copper nails in through, and it will hold the planks. If the nails were loose, the planks would work off with all the pounding of putting the others on. But I have it so I can just barely drive the nails in and that holds enough. This way the whole boat is planked first and then we rivet 'em all."

Stevens and a helper rivetted the *Evelyn* in two days, but a larger boat like the *Kathi Anne* or the *Margaret Anne* took four. "I used to count the number of times that I hit the nail, on the inside to rivet her, and I knew the number of nails in a rib and the number of ribs, and by multiplying — I think there were a hundred or more ribs into her — in four days, I hit with the hammer about a hundred thousand times."

This is not the only time I wonder at the pure physical stamina of this man in his midseventies. One of Nason's longer sequences is a medium close shot of Stevens with a small finishing adze, like a hand axe but with the blade turned the other way, chopping at the leading edge of the stem piece. The stem, once fitted into the keel assembly, presents a rectangular edge perhaps an inch and a half thick. The two sides of the hull converge into the stem piece, which must be shaved to a sharp knife edge that cuts the water. Stevens stands to one side of the bow and swings the adze in short, rhythmic strokes from head to belt height. The blade comes down with unflinching accura-

The completed hull.

cy in the slot of the previous blow, so that, as I watch, a single chip of wood the width of the stem curves outward as if animated and slowly peels off. The action seems as easy as peeling an orange, but if there is a misblow the stem cannot be removed and replaced. A New England boatbuilder, Dana Story, has written that a good adze man can finish a piece of wood to the smoothness of a grand piano with these blows.

I am struck by Stevens' face as he chips away at the stem, and stop the machine in order to study it in snapshot. It has become longer, drawn downward by his concentration, all the wrinkles smoothed out. The two force lines, those lines from the flange of the nose to the ends of the mouth that actors emphasize with makeup when playing heroic parts, are deeply drawn, as are the concentration lines from the ends of the mouth downward, and there is a slight furrow between his eyes, a furrow that I recognize later in his twenty-five-year-old grandson, Peter. But his forehead, the areas around the eyes, and the cheeks are all smooth, washed out by the work very nearly to the complexion of a boy. I start the machine again and count the number of blows in a sequence — 29 — 40 — 22 —

38 — 36 blows at a time, as he chips away, the muscles going on forever, a great peacefulness in his face.

"I don't know how he thought he would live when he retired," Dorothy says, recalling the days from 1969 to 1972 when Stevens worked alone on the *Kathi Anne*. "I know he had two thousand dollars in the bank — he said that recently — and his vegetable garden and his beeves. It would take an awful lot of hardship before Daddy would starve. And he was fortunate and sold some land, but before that, really, he was broke. Well, he's independent. Money doesn't play as much of a role in his life as for the rest of us. You see, he really built the *Kathi Anne* for himself. He had no intention of selling her."

Mary Dauphinee remembers his rekindled spirit at that time. "He was so *fascinated* with it. 'Mary,' he used to say, 'I can't wait to get out of bed in the morning and into the shop, I'm so excited about this boat.' " Each morning after the milking and the farm chores were done, he went to the shop, silent since the night before, the tools where he had left them at dusk, sawdust inches deep on the floor, and took up the next lumber for the *Kathi Anne*.

In a book called *The Atlantic Schooner*, written by Admiral H. F. Pullen for the schooner-building project at Expo '67, Stevens is quoted on how he proceeds at this stage of construction, when the boat is planked. "We start on the inside of the hull with the accommodations, which include bunks, galley, toilet, and so on, before the deck beams go on. That way you have more room to work. The inside gunwales are usually pieces of two-by-six shaped some and they are clamped in place and fastened with a bolt through each timber [rib] head. On top of that we step down about two inches and put in another piece about two inches square, which serves as a shelf strake and this is also bolted through planking, ribs and inside gunwales, with a nut on the inside.

"Now the deck beams are placed on top of this strip and also bolted down through, which makes a very secure job, I would say." [On a rough day during the schooner races, when the *Kathi Anne* is bucking into waves above head height, the horizon disappearing in each trough, and the whole man-made world seems very fragile, these words will come back to comfort me.]

"After the deck beams are in place, we knee them off in certain places for strength. Then we put in the mast bracing, which is usually made up of two-inch oak and put in what is known as a mast step. It is usually fastened with one-half-inch bronze bolts; then when that is done we put in the decking. Now it's a matter of choice what decking you use; we have been using groove and tongue pine about seven-eighths inch thick and covering it with canvas."

["Do you ever use plywood?"

Stevens gives me a disapproving look. "In the galley, I believe the bottom of the *Kathi Anne*'s dish rack is plywood."]

"After the decking is completed, we put on all the outside trim, such as the cabin house and safety rails. The sandpapering of the hull comes next, cleaning her up and sanding her well. The paint is applied in different colors and then she is about ready for out of the shop.

"Then we start on the rigging end of it, which includes making the spars and rigging. Most masts today are made out of sitka spruce and a lot of them are hollow, but we have been putting in solid spruce masts. We usually go into the woods and cut them, take them to the mill and have them four-squared; then from there we taper them up and round them up and sand them well and then comes the rigging.

"Then we launch her; set up the masts; set up all the rigging, try the sails on, and after that she's ready for the sea."

For the building of the *Kathi Anne*, the "we's" in this narrative had become "I's", and it took him two years to accomplish the tasks he so easily described. When asked about this, he replies, as if excuse were needed, "I wasn't working steady at it."

He decided to name the boat for his eldest granddaughter, Katherine Anne Peill, a blond young woman then sixteen years old. (It is Stevens' story that another of his granddaughters was miffed at this, so he found it necessary to build the *Mora* and the *Margaret Anne* to make all even.) Ten years before, he had built a forty-two-foot schooner and named it *Kathi Anne* after the same first grandchild, before selling it to a local yachtsman, so the new boat became officially *Kathi Anne II*.

Early in July 1972, the back doors of the small, barn-like shop were swung open and the hull of the *Kathi Anne* appeared, held upright by a cradle of two-by-six planks that rode on two skids held together by more planks, forming a rough sled. Stevens was on the seat of one of his farm machines, an old bulldozer, to which the sled was tied with a length of rope. The *Kathi Anne* moved carefully out into the sunlight and began the two-hundred-yard descent over the fields to the rim of Backman's Bay on the isthmus. The bulldozer's treads bit into the earth, trampling grass and turning up clods, its engine making growling and splatting sounds in the open air, but in a matter of ten minutes the procession had reached the brown sand of the shore.

The whole immediate family had come for the launch, and the group on the beach kept growing as bathers gathered and sightseers driving down the road pulled their cars up to the low dunes and joined the crowd, until thirty-five or forty people had collected. "People certainly come in when they see something like that going on."

The cradle was pointed toward the water and loaded with beach rocks on all its horizontal surfaces, so that, pushed down into the water by the bulldozer, the cradle would stay on the bottom while the hull floated free. Katherine Anne Peill stood to one side holding a bottle containing fruit juices that Evelyn Stevens had prepared — "We don't deal with strong liquors" — and at a signal from her grandfather broke it over the bronze fitting for the bow stay.

It is an old mariner's tale that a boat that swings eastward at the moment of launch will have rough sailing. *Kathi Anne II* eased into the waters of Mahone Bay, then swung slowly toward the west, toward the sun and the houses of Second

Peninsula. It was July 8, 1972, less than a week before the annual races of the Nova Scotia Schooner Association, which would lead to the International Schooner Race between the champions of New England and Nova Scotia.

Schooner racing goes back more than a hundred years on the Nova Scotia coast, to the days of the "salt bankers," large fishing schooners, often 130 feet or more in length, that fished the Grand Banks off Newfoundland, salted their catches on board, and raced each other to the docks of Nova Scotia and New England. The practical prize was to be first in and get the best price before the wharves were awash with fish baskets. But it is likely, too, that there was an appetite for excitement among the men who had worked for weeks hauling nets in the cold, fog-dimmed waters off Newfoundland, the spur of competition added to the natural spur of going home.

The friendly rivalries of the salt bankers were formalized in 1920 when a Halifax newspaper company, the Herald Limited, put up the Colonial Fisheries Trophy for the competition between the best of the Nova Scotia and New England schooners. One rule was that a boat must be a genuine fishing schooner, having spent at least a season on the Banks.

"I think it came about partly because of the America's Cup races," says Peter Brown, operations manager of *Bluenose II*, the replica of Canada's most famous racing schooner. "Those races were among those fragile, great J-Boats of the Vanderbilts and the Thomas Liptons. They were huge, great things, very expensive, the state of the art in their day — but they could never go out in very strong winds. The fishermen, who were out all the time in the North Atlantic, were somewhat contemptuous of these rich men and their monstrous toys. And I think they said, Let's show 'em how it's done, boys. And they set up their own races. Later, Thomas Lipton himself, Sir Thomas Lipton from England, became so interested in the fishing races that he put up the Lipton Cup."

The first International Race, in 1920, was won by the

American schooner *Esperanto*, out of Gloucester, Massachusetts, but the Canadians already had a 143-foot challenger on the ways named *Bluenose*, designed by William Roue, an amateur marine architect and ginger ale bottler from Halifax, and under construction in Lunenburg. (The origin of the term "bluenose," the centuries-old nickname for Nova Scotia mariners, is unclear. One version, according to Peter Brown, is that the seamen in earlier times traditionally wore mittens that were dyed blue, and that rubbing their dripping noses with the wet mittens caused some of the dye to come off. Another is simply that they were blue with the cold.)

*Bluenose* was launched in 1921 and sent off for her qualifying fishing season on the Grand Banks. That fall she defeated the American defender, *Elsie*, bringing the International Cup back to Nova Scotia. She proceeded to best every American challenger and win every series but one over the next eighteen years, until she was retired from racing and sold to carry cargo in the West Indies. There she went aground off Haiti in 1946 and was lost. *Bluenose*'s image is familiar to every present-day Canadian. A relief picture of "a fishing schooner," the exact profile of her, is on the back of the Canadian dime.

In the Stevens dining room, above one of the sideboards, is a large, misty old photograph behind glass in a walnut frame. Halifax harbor in the 1920s shows small in the background; in the foreground are four large schooners, their leeward rails awash, their four panoplies of sail puffing out, describing a whole folio of diagonal arcs in the wind. "That's the elimination with the Nova Scotia boats to pick out a winner," Stevens explains, "and of course the *Bluenose* won over the other three. My dad was sail trimmer onto her for that race."

"Sail trimmer?"

"It was his responsibility to set the sails on each tack, to get maximum advantage of the wind."

"Then he would be a pretty crucial man in a race."

"Yes, he would."

Dorothy Peill is more explicit, "He was sail trimmer on all the *Bluenose* races. The one series she didn't win was when

Grandpop was taken off down in Boston with an appendix about to burst. The saying here is, the man who trims the sails is the man who wins the race."

I look back at the picture, "Which one is the *Bluenose*?"

"The lead one, of course."

When *Bluenose* was lost in Caribbean waters it was felt deeply by many of the boatbuilders and sailors along the coast. After a long and frustrating campaign, they induced a private business, the Oland Brewery in Halifax, to put up the money to commission an exact replica of *Bluenose*, built from the original plans, in the same Lunenburg shipyard and by many of the same men. In 1963, *Bluenose II* was launched into Lunenburg harbor and proved to be as beautiful and swift as her namesake. Later donated to the Province of Nova Scotia, she is now berthed in Halifax during the summer, running excursions for visitors, and during the other seasons ranges the Atlantic coast and the Great Lakes as Canada's representative wherever the tall ships gather. Most North Americans who have a television set have watched the parade of sail of the tall ships at one or another of the Atlantic ports during the past decade. *Bluenose II* looks small next to some of the towering three-, four-, and five-masted boats from Europe and South America, but there is no mistaking her grace, her knife-smooth schooner profile, as she sails by the piled up canvas of the square riggers.

*Bluenose II* is an anachronism; there is no longer any need for 140-foot schooners on the Grand Banks, and there are no longer competitors for her to race. She sails the Atlantic waters like a constitutional monarch, dignified, unchallenged, expensive, a locus of pride and nostalgia.

But the love for schooners persists on the South Shore as well as at a number of ports along the New England coast, and smaller versions continue to be built for pleasure sailing — and probably as much as anything for the pure joy of the schooner's aesthetics. No other sailing boat has lines quite as balletic, as reminiscent of dancers, racehorses, whippets — that special category of living things that triumph over our normal gravity and inertia. No other sailing boat has her long sweep of hull echoed and amplified by the series of fore-and-aft-rigged sails lying close to it, repeating in the many curves of the canvas the curves of its wood. With all her sails and topsails set, her shoulder to the wind on a close reach, she has the look not just of a gull, but of a whole company of gulls riding high on the wind. Harry Bruce, a newspaperman and friend of David Stevens, describes it feelingly: "Schooners have a strange air of dignity, power and lyricism, and it's all their own. Somewhere, you may have met a woman who was so beautiful and poised you could scarcely open your mouth. A schooner under full sail is more like her than other boats are." Stevens says it with humor, looking out over the waters of the cove to where the *Kathi Anne* with her old-fashioned rigging rides stately at anchor, "She's the closest thing to a human being that a man can build."


Schooner sailing for pleasure became popular on the South Shore in the early 1960s, at first because there were so many old fishing schooners about. "The whole coast was just peppered with schooners," says Mort Pelham, for many years secretary of the Nova Scotia Schooner Association. "People were buying them up for four or five hundred dollars and converting them to pleasure boats." The association was founded at Hubbards in 1961 when eleven owners met aboard the schooner *Adare*, herself a fisherman built on Tancook Island in the first decade of the century. "See, our idea then was to do research and make records of all the schooners before they passed out of existence. The object wasn't just racing." He points to the constitution of the Schooner Association, which lists as its objectives: "To preserve, maintain and further interest in Nova Scotia schooners of all types" and "To collect all possible information on schooners, their builders, owners, histories, pictures. . . ." The third objective decrees that schooner races be held at least once a year, "to determine the Nova Scotia Schooner Championship." However, the fourth pledges "To stimulate the design and construction of schooner-type vessels."

It was this fourth objective that brought about a new wave of business for David Stevens, his cousins the Heislers, the Masons, and other South Shore boatbuilders. "As a result of the association and these races," Pelham says, "quite a number of new schooners were built. I would say about twenty were built at that time, as pleasure boats, not as fishing boats."

Stevens built his first schooner in 1950, a thirty-six-footer for a Miss McCormick, who was a summer resident of Chester. In the decade that began in 1961, when the Schooner Association was founded, he built nine more before starting on the *Kathi Anne*, and most of them were sailed in the annual Schooner Race Week. Each year in the third week of July schooners appear from as far down the coast as Barrington Passage, one hundred miles away, and as far to the east as Halifax, to race at the Hubbards, Lunenburg or La Have River yacht clubs, for a series of silver cups, trays and other trophies — the Oland Tray, the Admiral Pullen Trophy (named for a charter member), the MacAskill Trophy, the Premier's Cup (usually presented by a local politician), the Colonial Fisheries Trophy (won by the original *Bluenose*), the Old Gaffers Trophy — and in recent years, the Stevens Trophy, for a race exclusively among the owners of schooners built by David Stevens.

The revived schooner races had been going on for nine years when, in the spring of 1970, the publisher of the Halifax newspaper announced a revival of the traditional rivalry that made *Bluenose* famous: he would put up a trophy for a schooner championship to be sailed between New England and Nova Scotia. The New England champion would be the winner of the Great Schooner Races in Gloucester, the Nova Scotia champion to be selected in a series of three races during Schooner Race Week.

Stevens received the news as he was planking the still-skeletal hull of the *Kathi Anne*, but if he had any thoughts of competing in the revived international race when the *Kathi*

*Anne* was completed he did not reveal them. Although he has raced sailing boats all his life, he is a quiet man and does not seem at first meeting particularly competitive. He shares the Canadian diffidence that could almost be called a national trait: a dislike of fuss that instructs strangers, especially newspaper and television reporters, not to make too much of things, a sense of proportion and a sense of accuracy. (An example of Nova Scotian accuracy: Peter Brown's story of an early-morning encounter on the Lunenburg wharf between a visitor from Ontario and an old man jigging a hand fishing line. Visitor: "Have you lived here all your life?" Old fisherman: "Not yet.") These qualities add up to a sense of realism so strong, so precise, so at ease with the immediate day that you wonder if they ever dream, these realistic Canadians — you wonder what it is that makes them race.

But of course David Stevens does dream; his line of seventy boats was not built by engineering. "He works with a *passion*," Mary Dauphinee says. "When he was seven years old I knew he was going to be a boatbuilder. He would sit in our kitchen with his jackknife and whittle out a little mold from wood, so his toy boat would have a lead keel just like his grandfather's boats. And he'd find odds and ends of lead, put them in a pot, start up the stove to melt them down. Mother would say, 'Children, get out of the way!' when he was carrying the hot lead to the mold. He was so demanding, so insistent," she says with a mixture of resentment and pride. "Everything was pushed aside. Today a child like that would be thought of as a genius."

Whatever the burden of that passion that made him, in Mary's words, "a different child altogether," at the age of seventy-six, Stevens seems to have it well under control. When he talks of racing his tone is so casual he might be discussing turnip cultivation or the advantages of one type of cattle feed over another. "No," he says, leaning back in a lawn chair set to catch the afternoon sun, "they're getting so taken on *winning*. No, one of my main objectives is to teach my grandsons to be good losers. That's part of the game. If you can't do that, then don't race." After a moment's thought, the eyes glint and he adds, "And of course, there's always the wind."

A few minutes later, recalling the schooner races the previous month at Shelburne, he talks not of the two trophies he brought home but of the fact that in one race he passed *Sebim*, his old rival, "my keenest competitor," to windward, beating her close-hauled, the most demanding tack for skipper and boat. "That was my greatest satisfaction," he says with an open grin.

Competitive or not, Stevens has a strong sense of fairness and of the rules by which the game is played. The *Kathi Anne*'s seams had barely had time to swell when he took her out on a Saturday afternoon in July 1972 for her one and only shakedown sail. The next evening he attended the skippers meeting at the Lunenburg Yacht Club to go over the rules of the elimination trials for the International Race, and found an unexpected obstacle. "I didn't have any equipment, no food, water or anything aboard, nothing. And they were going to disqualify me."

"On what grounds?"

"That I wasn't outfitted. We had to be equipped for five men to go to sea for five days. Well, I knew that was true for international racing, but I didn't think it was true for just the elimination races here and they hung that over my head. And I said well it's impossible almost to get this boat ready for tomorrow morning at ten o'clock. So I went home and all my family gathered round and we said, we'll fix that. We got up at five o'clock on Monday morning and we went at it, family and friends, loaded in food and water and wood, got the engine wired up and everything working. And by ten o'clock we were ready."

In the elimination races, Stevens found himself up against *Adare*, a schooner owned by Victor Oland, the millionaire Halifax brewery owner and then lieutenant governor of Nova Scotia. *Adare* was sailed, in the old yachting tradition, by a fessional crew; *Kathi Anne* by a collection of Stevens' relatives, neighbors, college boys and her nameling, Katherine Anne Peill.

A correspondent for the Canadian edition of *Time* magazine, James Wilde, described the third race of the series: "The morning of the final, decisive trial, Stevens, as always, milked his cows and contemplated strategy. . . . The first day, *Kathi Anne II* lost out on the 30-mi. course by 1 min. and 30 sec. She won the second race, this time 25 miles, by a slim 27-sec. margin. 'Don't mind if I'm a bit growly today,' he joked. 'We've beaten *Adare* once and they are out for blood today, boys.'

"His spatulated fingers caressing the tiller, Stevens was as calm and self-assured as the still sea when the starting gun fired. Only the darting, blue-gray eyes betrayed [his] obsessive desire to win. . . . A combination of superb sailing and sharp sail handling sent her breezing along the 22-mi. course and across the finish line almost a full 4 min. ahead of the rival *Adare*. As Stevens' other grandchildren stood on shore, waving a white sheet for a victory symbol, he exuberantly shouted 'better luck next time' to the vanquished crew."

Stevens and the *Kathi Anne* and the motley Stevens crew then went against the American champion, *Outward Bound*, a schooner based in Boston. They beat her two races straight—in one race finishing a full hour ahead of the American. *Kathi Anne* was seventeen days old and an international champion. Skipper David Stevens was sixty-five years old and sailing his sixty-fifth boat—the first one he had built alone. "After that," he said, clearly remembering a day in his shop three years before, "the young fellows took a second look at 'the old man.' "

"That is what made it so sweet to him," Dorothy says, "for the old man who was ready to swallow the anchor—to come up with a winner like her."

Over the next five years, *Kathi Anne* defended the trophy three more times against American challengers, *Amberjack* in

1973, *Agamemnon* in 1974, and *Alicia* in 1977, winning against all, in some cases by embarrassingly wide margins. In other years, *Sebim* won the right to defend for Nova Scotia, and has also bested the Americans, who have yet to win the International Trophy. "*Sebim* has won it three times, although once there were no eliminations. She just showed up over in Gloucester and raced. *Kathi Anne* has won it four times. That's the most," he says with open satisfaction, "since the *Bluenose*."

In August 1974, in a moment of uncharacteristic bravado, Stevens even challenged *Bluenose II* to race the *Kathi Anne*. The occasion was the awards ceremony at the Lunenburg Yacht Club, where he received the International Trophy for the third time, having beaten *Agamemnon*, a graceful, black-hulled schooner out of Miami and Nassau, in two consecutive races. *Agamemnon's* skipper was present, as were Stevens' regular racing partners, the yacht owners of Halifax and the South Shore. He had just been handed the weighty, Empire-style silver cup by the representative of the Halifax *Herald Limited*, and in his acceptance remarks almost casually mentioned that the taxpayers, who owned the *Bluenose II*, might like to see their boat, like her famous predecessor, in the role of racing schooner.

The next day the Halifax newspaper headlined an article, "Stevens Challenges *Bluenose II*"—but no one that evening took the suggestion seriously. Every boatman knows what Stevens would be the first to point out—the longer a boat is in the water, the faster she sails, and *Kathi Anne*, thirty-one feet at the waterline, was in fact as much challenger for the 112-foot *Bluenose II* as a scrappy terrier would be for a greyhound. The challenge, everyone present knew, was Stevens' humor, a quiet way of expressing the elation he felt over a string of victories that had not been matched since the 1920s. They also knew that he was entitled—that a month earlier, when he walked down to the road one morning to his battered aluminum mailbox, he had found an official-looking envelope from

Ottawa, and in it notification that he had been named by Queen Elizabeth as a member of the Order of Canada, his country's democratic equivalent of the royal honors list.

"I'm not beat yet!"

We turn away from the dual stump and walk back toward the curtain of light at the edge of the wood. This time I have no trouble keeping up with Stevens' usual, measured stride. "There's maple growing here," he says, looking at some thin saplings at the line of the barbed wire. "I'd forgotten we had maple coming along." As we walk back across the nibbled pasture behind the Stevens barn and boatshop, one of the fly-covered Guernseys trundles up to us with that unpredictable curiosity that afflicts one cow out of a grazing herd. The sky is now the full blue of midmorning. Off to the left, the surface of Mahone Bay, roughed by the wind, reflects back a deeper blue. Around the head of Big Tancook, six miles distant, tall white sails have appeared, seeming motionless as clouds in the patch of morning haze that still clings to the water.

"Chester Race Week," Stevens says. "They'll be out there most of the day."

Across the pasture to meet us come a slim, brown-haired young woman and two young men in bib overalls, one dark with a mustache and a serious, slightly frowning expression, the other with a head of bushy blond hair and an equally bushy mustache. The dark young man is Peter Peill, a Stevens grandson; the others, Norwood and Uta Kungle, are a newly-married couple, immigrants from Germany who work on the Peill farm in the Annapolis Valley, an hour's drive to the north. They have appeared, as members of the Stevens clan do, because there is work on the schedule this morning—a cradle down at the mooring by the homestead must be repaired and set in the water for the next high tide, so the *Pocahontas* can be hauled up for repairs. Introductions are made and we stand in the reflecting warmth of the pasture for a moment, discussing the repair job. Then Stevens goes into the boatshop and reappears with a hammer, the only tool he will take with him. He climbs onto the seat of his tractor and invites us to perch on the open frame of the trailer, which is piled haphazardly with boards.

"Now if you fall off and kill yourselves, don't sue me for damages," he calls over the sound of the engine, and we lurch off down the driveway, the boards moving under us like a mechanical horse. Turning down the hill toward Backman's Bay, we are sitting so low on the lumber that the perhaps ten-mile-an-hour speed of the tractor makes the road surface flow by in a blur.

The ride in the open air is exhilarating, the sky streaked with whitewash clouds, the cool drink of the morning air, the brilliant yellows and oranges of the flowerbeds as we cross the sandy isthmus and come up the hill past Wilfrid Stevens' well-tended house, past Marie Stevens Harnish's house and flowerbeds. It all seems freshly created on this August morning—the free world of David Stevens.

The pavement stops at the sail loft, R. B. Stevens and Co., Ltd. The doors to the cellar are open—the cellar that David and his father dug by hand, under the loft, two years after it was built.

Someone, a man in a plaid shirt, is bringing crates of cabbages up and loading them into the trunk of a car.

# TANCOOK

$A$t ten minutes to ten the next morning the horn of the Tancook Ferry sends out warning blasts that bounce like flat stones off the waters of Chester harbor and lift over the still town. A few yachtsmen are on the town wharf, dressed in suntan slacks and sneakers and white or navy Irish cable pullovers against the cool morning air. They talk in small groups, sometimes pointing out over the city of sloops spread southwest on the surface of the harbor, their masts an antenna farm in the reddish sunlight. Beyond the bridge to the peninsula more masts crowd the back harbor.

At the business end of the wharf, men dressed in green workshirts and trousers connect the cables to lift grey, rectangular cargo boxes onto the stern deck of the ferry. The boxes are hoisted by a telescope-arm crane mounted just aft of the pilot house on the top deck. I watch a five-foot square box marked "Mail" being swung onto the stern and wonder at the number of letters, or perhaps mail orders, that would go to

Tancook. The crane arm returns with a whine to the dock and the cables are arranged to lift a small boat trailer and the metal rowboat upturned on it. On the top deck, the first mate oversees the loading. He is dressed in the black trousers, light grey, short-sleeved shirt, black tie and peaked cap that Canadian officials of all sorts—policemen, customs officers, mailmen, park rangers—seem to wear with such good-natured ease. Uniformed life, stretching up the chain of command to the captain, is natural in seafaring country; uniformed life stretching back across the ocean to the figure of the Queen, or in other days the King, is still natural in a country that for centuries has been a part of empire.

The third and predominant population of the wharf is dressed in bright sweaters, canvas shoes, plaid shorts and culottes, denim skirts and blond slacks, sunglasses, a variety of caps, usually of woven plastic, slung cameras, tote bags. They are the visitors set for a day's excursion to Big Tancook Island, and we are among them.

Bart and Francine Shea, a couple in their early thirties, are part of David's crew; they sailed with him in the Shelburne races the previous month. Their two boys, Liam and Brian, eight and twelve, are already on board, checking over the decks and the hidden corners of the boat. Evelyn Stevens is well prepared for travel, with a substantial cardigan sweater, a raincoat, a kerchief for her hair, and is carrying several bags that seem to be filled with food and house presents for the people we are going to visit. David is the most formally dressed of all of us, wearing a trim new tweed jacket and trousers that are plumb-line creased. He has the look, not surprisingly, of a retired sea captain, relaxed but instinctively more comfortable in a tailored jacket than in the easy freedom of polyesters. Then too, the others in the cheerful, laden crowd that works its way along the gangplank are outward bound. David is returning home.

The ferry is a motor craft of the Province of Nova Scotia, about seventy feet long, painted white with three black stripes along the side, one at the edge of the top deck where passengers can stand at the rail and enjoy the view, one below the windows of the enclosed deck where people sit on installed benches at tables, and the third at the waterline. The afterdeck is open and broad like a Cape Island boat, looked over by the head and neck of the loading crane. As I come up the gangway and step onto the metal deck with its elephant skin of paint I am reminded again of what a metal universe the modern boat has become — the Age of Steam was also the Age of Iron. Even the few bits of wooden rail and the carpeting that soften the passenger areas are simply laid over the bolted and welded steel. Through the soles of my shoes I feel the engines humming, and know that every light socket, guard rail, bulkhead, hull plate and window frame is vibrating too.

Evelyn and Francine have settled themselves at the first table in the cabin, the carrying bags crowded around them, and are contending with questions from the boys. David, at a corner of railing on the upper deck just aft of the pilothouse, is inspecting the sloops in the harbor. To the right is one particularly tall mast that clears the air above all the others.

"That's the *Hayseed*," David says when I point her out. "She's the scratch boat for Race Week." He explains that the races involve more than a hundred sloops of varying lengths and classes, so that once their ratings or handicaps are applied, the first boat across the finish line is rarely the winner. The scratch boat, the largest and therefore the fastest, is the boat used as the standard to rate all the others, which are given time allowances — to come up to scratch.

The horn of the ferry sounds a final time and the engines rise to a level that momentarily blots out conversation. The forest of masts begins to rotate as the boat backs away from the wharf in an arc, pulling its bow around toward the light blue haze of Mahone Bay. The vibration stops for a moment and then begins again in earnest as the boat starts forward. The wharf slips away behind us, and the broader view of the town appears, mostly trees and roofs, here and there a patch of Chester white clapboard. On both sides of us, on the peninsula to our left and on the high ground leading to Nauss Point on our right, large white mansions look out from among the trees—four-square, formal, 1920s Georgian, housing third generations, keeping watch on the ocean and the dignity of the bay.

There is no wind, and as we watch our wake turning precise furrows in the glassy water, David is reminded of the last winter his family spent on the island.

"This was all solid," he swings an arm forward in the direction of the open water. "It was so cold in February—1919 that was—the bay froze. People would walk back and forth to Chester on the ice."

I look at the widening plane of Mahone Bay spreading out into the haze of the Atlantic Ocean. "This whole thing froze over?"

"Well, you know it had to be cold to freeze salt water, but there was no wind. If the wind comes in from the southeast," he gestures a few degrees off the bow, "you'd get these long rolling swells that would break everything up. But it just happened that February there were no storms, absolutely no wind—everything still and silent."

He looks out at the glassy water which, but for the booming of the ship's engines, would be as silent this morning, and talks about the last winter they spent on Tancook, and about the islanders' self-sufficiency. Everyone raised their own vegetables, and cabbages for sauerkraut, the cash crop. Tancook sauerkraut was famous.

"And they raised the best beef in the world because the land was so rich."

"I thought it was a rocky island."

"It is. There's only about a foot of soil all over the island. All the rest is solid rock. Lots of times the plow would strike into solid rock. But that keeps all the natural fertilizers right up to the surface. Oh, the land was very fertile. During the tourist season, the butcher in Chester told me he would never buy beef from any other place than Tancook. In those days, I bet there were 180 cattle on the island, because every man had at least a team—either a single ox or a pair of oxen—that he worked. Plowed his field, pulled the wagons."

"Did they use horses?"

"No man could afford a horse. Expensive to buy, and if anything happened to him, a dead loss."

"Dead loss?"

"With oxen you could work them, and then they were beef. If a horse died, it was a dead loss."

Later he talks about his grandfather's boatyard on Tancook and what a fascination it was for a seven-year-old.

"They couldn't keep me away from it. I'd come home from school—I must have been seven or eight years old—and I wouldn't even go in the house. Just throw my book bag over the fence, and I'd sneak into the boatshop. I was just possessed by a need to get at tools. I'd get a piece of wood and take my grandfather's spokeshave, and I'd start chipping away. First thing he'd come around and see me. He'd yell at me, 'Put that tool down, you're dulling it.' I'd lay it down and sulk a little bit—but when he'd go around the other side of the boat I'd be back at it again. I used to get what my mother called 'the nine o'clock sickness'—too sick to go to school but by nine o'clock I'd be sitting up in bed and calling for her to go down to the boatshop and bring me a piece of pine, to whittle a model."

"How did she take to that?"

"Well," he smiles, "she got to know all the woods."

"Hello David, how are you?" The greeting comes from a trim, tanned man in ship's uniform who has appeared around the corner of the deckhouse.

"Oh, hi," David greets him pleasantly but with an edge of reserve. He is searching for the name.

"You're looking good."

"Oh, feel pretty good."

"You know me."

"Oh yes." There is a pause.

"I'm a Stevens."

"Yes," David says with more enthusiasm; he has found the name. "Arthur." He begins a round of introductions. Arthur Stevens identifies himself as the first mate of the boat and, although he looks thirty-five at most, says that he has been sailing as mate for seventeen years.

"Are you related?" I ask, "or is everyone around here just named Stevens?"

"Well yes, we're related. We're all related, really. I was just talking about it back on the wharf to a couple of fishermen — the Stevenses — that we all originated from two. There were two Stevenses that came from Scotland."

"Oh no, you're wrong there," David puts in. "They came from Germany."

"Oh? Germany?"

"The name was originally Stuebing. Johannes Stuebing, I think. Came to Lunenburg. May have been a Hessian soldier. Name was changed somewhere along the line."

Arthur Stevens looks a bit doubtful at the sudden change of his lineage, but David has some history on his side. Lunenburg County was settled by German immigrants imported by the new British establishment in Halifax in 1753 as a population buffer against the French Acadians, the original settlers of the colony. (The British military "solved" the French problem by force two years later with the expulsion of thousands of Acadian families and their dispersal along the Atlantic seaboard from New England to Louisiana, a story made famous by Longfellow's poem, "Evangeline.") Today names like Swicker, Wolff, Kaulback, Finck and Schultz are common in Lunenburg and identify the original owners of many of the town's historic houses. But the population of the province is still predominately English, Scotch, and Scotch-Irish, and the other members of David Stevens' family generally trace their lineage to New England and the loyalist emigration to Nova Scotia in 1783. It is one of David's singularities that he denies out of hand any British heritage, and extolls the virtues of the "German turnip farmers" who settled Lunenburg County, broke the land with ox teams, were "thrifty as all get-out," worked hard, were good citizens — until, he notes, the rum running started in the 1920s. He generally praises anything

German or connected with Germany. When his son, Murray, graduated from high school in 1956, he sent him to Germany to learn stainless steel welding for the boat trade, convinced that he would learn there the most advanced techniques. "The German people, you know, have to be pretty sound."

His daughter, Dorothy, is married to Jurgen Peill, an engineer from a family of agricultural and industrial entrepreneurs in Germany, and they have a prosperous farm and seed business at Canning in the Annapolis Valley. The family story is that David discouraged the local suitors to his daughter. When he met young "Jock" Peill, who came to see him about pulpwood to export to Germany, they talked until midnight, and when Dorothy got off the train from Halifax the next Friday, he announced, "I've met the man you can marry."

"Oh have you?" was her reply.

Dorothy tells the story now with high humor and not a trace of resentment. "I had enough sense — the only sense I had was that Daddy, I felt, knew men better than I did. But at the time, it kind of annoyed me. Nobody had ever been good enough. So he invited Jock to dinner that Sunday and I invited five girlfriends down from Halifax. I thought, this guy is going to be shown right off the bat that I'm not interested. We were upstairs when he arrived, looking out the window, and I took one look and said, 'Girls, you stay right here!' So I went down and we met — and you know, I suppose once in a lifetime, if you're lucky, it simply happens. We looked at each other and I don't think there was ever any question." She laughs delightedly at the irony. "It was unbelievable! Down here on Second Peninsula he found a real, true-blooded Kraut from Germany! It was like the moon in his hand."

"Johannes Stuebing came from Germany," David repeats, "in, I think, 1790."

"Well, the reason I say that," Arthur persists, "my sister has a book at home — that has the whole history of all the Stevenses since the first one came. Well," he is not going to make an argument of it, "it may be a long way back, but we're all related anyway."

"Yes," David is agreeable to blurring the issue for courtesy's sake. "Maybe we're fourth or fifth cousins."

The horn of the boat sounds twice, and we look forward to see a concrete jetty on a low piece of shoreline covered with grey brush. There are a few houses scattered back from the shore, uncared for and seeming for the most part uninhabited. The brightly dressed passengers are at the rail looking down at the workmen waiting for lines from the boat.

"Little Tancook," Arthur announces and disappears around the corner of the deckhouse.

During the unloading of some grey boxes from the after-deck, David strikes up a conversation with a slim young woman in her early thirties, dressed in the slacks, bright shirt and tote bag of a day-visitor. Her name is Connie and she is from Montreal, which starts David reminiscing about the building of the *Atlantica* at Expo '67. Admiral Pullen, who set up the schooner-building project, ordered David to work on Sunday, the day of the largest crowds at the exposition. David's religious convictions are only rarely and indirectly expressed—"I wasn't going to . . . set a bad example"—but are deeply held. He refused and almost walked away from the project, but the admiral backed down. "*So*, we went there and there wasn't a blow struck on Sunday! Not a blow! And we got her done on time."

Curious, and thinking it will interest Connie, I ask him about the day the Queen came to see the boat. I am remembering the photo in David's dining room, the boat's hull in the well, David in a dark suit, white shirt and tie, standing with Prussian formality in front of it.

"Yes, she was just planked up," he looks embarrassed and his casual manner comes over him like a disguise. "Well, the hostesses lined up—and so did I. And I was introduced to her . . . and then she went on, and then Prince Philip came back and I had a chat with him. He wanted to know the dimensions of the boat and so on."

"Did he go on board?"

"No. Just stopped for a moment to ask how long she was

and so on. Just a few questions. I don't remember them all now. And I answered them." Another pause.

"What was your impression of him?"

"Seemed all right. Those people are trained from the cradle right up — to be above all other people. I mean, to be superior."

"You felt they were being superior?"

"No, no. They didn't show it, but I know the training."

It is apparent that the training struck him as much as the royal couple, but beyond that, he will not be impressed — unlike Mary Dauphinee, who says with complete conviction, "The Queen. That was the ultimate recognition for our family."

For some minutes now the boat has been moving swiftly along the shore of Big Tancook Island. We can see the accuracy of David's description of the soil. The island as it dips down into the waters of the bay is igneous rock, the smoothly poured cap of molten rock that is so typical of Canada's shield country to the west. On top of that, a crust of yellow earth hardly more than a foot thick shows at the edges, where the waves have washed the rock clean — a pate of rock just barely topped with soil.

The houses are becoming more numerous as the boat moves along the shore toward the seawall that forms the harbor at Northwest Cove.

"There," David points over the rail, "there is where I lived — you see the blue house over there."

It is not difficult to pick out the blue house, a two-story rectangle of vivid cerulean blue with white trim, a flat roof and regular windows with mullions making white crosses in them — it stands out from the shoreline like a child's drawing of a house.

"The squarish one there?"

"The square one. But it's not exactly square either. And the schoolhouse is — was — right over there. You see this little island off here," he points off the starboard bow to a flat-topped mound of earth about a half mile off the shore. "That's Star Island. In order to prove you were a man down here you had to jump off the wharf and swim to that island and back, and then you had to take a barrel of flour, which was 198 pounds, and you had to put that on your shoulder and walk away with it."

I look at David's tough but small frame. He has never weighed close to 198 pounds in his life. "That's quite a task."

"Well I never got to the barrel," he says with a grin, "but I did make the swim." As the ferry approaches the seawall of the harbor, he points to a stretch of gravelly beach just where the concrete meets the land. "That's where my dad took me on my first swim as a little boy. I was stark naked and hanging onto his back, my arms around his neck, and he swam from there around the breakwater and into the harbor."

The concrete jetty, as we pass along its seawall side, is crowded with pickup trucks, a few cars among them. Giving festive blasts from its horn, the ferry swings 180 degrees around the end of the jetty, and we are suddenly in a tropical garden of boats. Cape Island boats, in violent yellow, blue, purple, red, green — every color of the rainbow — tied two or three abreast, line the inner angle of the jetty. At a floating dock extending into the center of the harbor from the land side are the pleasure boats — wood or fiberglass launches and power cruisers in more sedate whites and greens, except for one old peacock of a wooden ketch with a bright blue hull, bright yellow deck and cabin, and a sore-thumb orange life preserver.

Below us on the dock as we disembark are stacked blue plastic tubs full of flat silver flanges of cod, salted stiff. At the end of the gangplank we say goodbye to Connie and her husband, who has joined us during the last few minutes of the voyage, and tell them to enjoy Tancook, although looking up at the scattering of tight little houses on the hill above us — there is not even a store to mark the center of the community — I find it hard to imagine what they and this whole boatload of brightly plumed visitors will do with themselves. As it turns out, they are somehow magically absorbed by the island, for we do not see another tote bag or woven plastic cap or sweater tied around the waist all day. Melted into air—into thin air.

Our little band—two children, five adults, with coats and carry-all bags—threads its way among the crowd of pickup trucks. To our left on the bay side is a concrete wall just at eye height, to keep the waves from washing equipment off the dock. Winter storms can be intense—David says his grandmother once got seasick walking along the shore road during a winter storm. At the base of the wall collections of buoys lie on their sides, at the tops of their shafts little aluminum flags in the shape of two intersecting diamonds. The same diamonds top the masts of the Cape Island boats, and David explains they are radar reflectors. Then I notice all the fishing boats are equipped with radar units, their curved horizontal bars looking futuristic against the old, frequently painted wood.

We reach the end of the jetty and walk into a cloud of dust stirred up by a girl on a motorbike. A few steps along the shore road we turn uphill on a steep weedy track worn by car tires. To the right, beyond a border of Queen Anne's lace and fireweed, is a broad fairway of a lawn which, on closer inspection, turns out to be mowed dandelions. At the top of the lawn, perched on the ridge overlooking the harbor, is a yellow house, quite raffish compared to the others we have spotted on Tancook. The roof edge across the front has a cheerful, scalloped trim, like a line of waves in a medieval painting. The four regularly set windows, however, are surmounted by small pediments that give a classical look. It is the only house on the island with trim, David tells us, and is the house where his mother was born.

On the lawn at the side of the house we meet Gilbert Slauenwhite, the present owner and the sixth generation of his family to occupy the house. Gilbert is tall, over six feet, black-haired, and appears to be in his midthirties. He has friendly lines around his eyes and across his forehead, and when he smiles, which he does frequently, the gap between his front teeth completes his charm. We are introduced to Goldie, his wife, a tall, strong-looking blond woman who immediately collects

Evelyn and her carry-alls and goes to see about dinner. The rest of us sit in a line along the ridge of the lawn, facing the harbor in a motley of lawn chairs, kitchen chairs with spokes missing and woven plastic pads set on the mowed dandelions. We talk back and forth along the line, as we would sitting at a counter, but at any pause in the conversation eyes turn naturally back to the harbor spread out below us and the wide blue haze of Mahone Bay beyond it. The view keeps entering the conversation in the pauses.

"What a difference since I was a boy," David says. "The harbor was all schooners."

He talks about boats getting stuck in the harbor mud. To get them off they would wait until the tide went out and tip them over, then the flood tide would float them again.

Gilbert says there are no fish this month. Normally off East Ironbound, an island on the ocean side, a boat could take several thousand mackerel a day. Now the nets are coming up empty.

There is a pause while our gazes turn back to the bay. The surface is so smooth the water is grey and oily-looking. David predicts there will be no wind, no race today for the Chester yachts.

Walter Cross, an old Tancook resident, is moving to the mainland, to join his children. The news surprises everyone and there are murmurs of protest.

The conversation ambles on, broken by pauses while we stare at the bay, and I realize we are doing something I remember from my youth, something much more common before the days of radio, television and other manufactured entertainments—we are visiting. It used to drive me crazy, sitting around when I was six years old, listening to the desultory talk of the great-aunts and great-uncles. Now the rhythm is soothing.

Gilbert talks about the Reef Woman, whom we will visit on our tour of the island after dinner. She is a college professor's wife who has restored a fisherman's cottage at a spot on the ocean side.

David recalls an old character they encountered on their visit last summer, a drunk who engaged him in a long, haranguing comparison of their ages. "Oh, he was a fierce old fellow."

Gilbert is asked about his garden. To one side he has corn, squash, cabbage, strawberries, carrots. On the other side of the house, a raspberry thicket, looking impenetrable as a hedgerow, runs down toward the shore. They picked five gallons there earlier in the week.

Gilbert discourses affectionately on his pickup truck, which is scheduled to take us on the tour of the island. She has four cylinders; two and a half work. Well, he left the key on for a couple of days, so that didn't do her any good, had to push her down the hill to get started. Someone approves of that and we see his gat-toothed smile. Only thing wrong was, she has no brakes.

Francine talks about the sail down the coast to Shelburne the previous month for the schooner races. She starts gently, then more openly kidding David about his old-fashioned ways and his disinclination to sail out of home waters. They rented a Loran C, a radio navigational device, for the trip. "David thought it was a sin," Francine says with a broad smile. David, unruffled, says dead reckoning is still pretty good. Francine accuses him of playing a string out the stern of the boat to find his way back to Second Peninsula and calls it the longest umbilical cord she ever saw. There is general laughter, from David too, who is kidded by very few people.

Gazes drift back to the harbor. David tells his father's story of a three-hundred-pound swordfish captured when it came into the harbor and got tangled in the seagrass. Gilbert says a fourteen-foot shark cruised the harbor last year.

Gilbert, Goldie and their children are on vacation. They live in Dartmouth, across the harbor from Halifax, where Gilbert has an industrial job, and come down here to the family homestead for a month each summer. This practice must be fairly recent because they are involved in a vigorous restoration of the house.

We get up from our comfortable chairs and pads on the lawn and circle the exterior. Most of the rococo trim on the roof edge, Gilbert shows us, is newly carved to replace what was rotting away. At the other end of the house, by the cellar door, the foundation stones have been remortared. David remembers pressing cabbage for sauerkraut in that cellar, in the same way that grapes were pressed for wine in Europe. "They washed my feet out here on the lawn, then carried me down the steps and into the tub."

It is time to go into the house, where two tables have been set together in the dining room to accommodate the crowd. The children are at one, the rest of us at the other. Heads are bowed by unspoken consent and David says a grace; then white bowls brimming with the garden are passed around— peas, squash, beans, potatoes, carrots, cucumber salad, and broad platters of fresh fried haddock. Goldie has not only prepared a feast but done it in a dry sink. There is as yet no running water in the house; everything is managed from the pump in the backyard, including pitchers of sweet iced tea at each end of the table. The food is plain and delicately cooked, its freshness as palpable as garlic. I think even those accustomed to midday dinners must be indulging a bit, for when the desert course comes, no one can make it to the second cake.

We drift slowly outside and surround Gilbert's truck that seems to be planted in the lawn near the tall grass at the back like a sturdy rust perennial. Both headlights are long since gutted and the hood of the engine has gone somewhere. The downhill door hangs open like a wounded arm. We begin removing the contents of the bed—rope, empty gas cans, old cable, a tire—carrying them up a few yards and dropping them out of sight in the tall grass, while Gilbert fiddles with the engine. He thinks aloud—charting his course around the island, he cheerfully informs us, to require the minimum use of brakes. After a few minutes of this and no sound from the engine, he disappears in the direction of the raspberry hedge. We stand around talking, one or another of us strolling over in turn to make use of the little upright house in the middle of the back lawn. In ten minutes Gilbert is back, driving across the lawn in a pristine red pickup without a wear mark on it. He has thought better of the brake situation and borrowed his neighbor's new truck for the excursion. We go back to the tall grass and search out a bench and boxes, retrieve the tire, and arrange them in the spotless bed of the new truck as seats. As the visitor, and perhaps the tenderfoot, I am offered a place in the cab with Gilbert and Evelyn, but insist on riding in the back with David, Bart, Francine and the boys. With an exuberant shout from our tour director we bounce over the lawn and down the hill to the shore road.

Our immediate destination is the "backalong," the other settled area, along the edge of the southeast cove, about a mile across the high center of the island. For people in the settlement by the harbor this was once a journey. "You might almost be grown," David says, "before you got to the backalong. Little girls would say, When I grow up, I want to go to the backalong."

From the west end of the harbor the dirt road goes up a steep hill past the Tancook post office, the seat of government and the one place where the name is displayed in these little towns without commercial signs. To our right a high point out into Mahone Bay is covered with dense pines, but the rest of the land is rolling brown field grass or boggy-looking vetch, with an occasional thorn bush taking the land back from the absent cattle. As we come down a rise to a spot where the road forks, David points to a copse of spindly locust to the right of the road. "That's where my father saw the ghost." Walking along this road one night the young Randolph Stevens had been startled and chilled by a figure in white moving through the woods. It was an exciting encounter for a boy, but, grown and more experienced, he had decided it was the white shirt of someone leaving his girlfriend's house later than he wanted to be seen.

The first houses of the backalong appear on either side of the road and we pull in the driveway of a spruce white bungalow with bright flowerbeds. A woman is in the front yard, mowing the already neatly cropped lawn. We disembark over the sides of the truck and meet the wife of Walter Cross, who is out at the moment. News is exchanged standing on the side lawn, and they discuss the Crosses' forthcoming move to the mainland in a tone of surprise, almost as if they would like to argue with her, but in the manner of older people who arrange their lives carefully, the Crosses are not sentimental about the change. "Walter says he was born on the island, it doesn't mean he has to die on it." That brings the subject to a close. She takes us to the barn at the end of the driveway and into a shed room at the side where two long tables are covered with carved birds, Walter's hobby in retirement. The song birds, perched on branches and twigs, are mostly bright; the ducks, mergansers and larger water birds are painted realistically, like decoys. Francine buys a handsome pair of blue-winged teal and I buy a large, bright-eyed loon that reminds me of the one that visits our bay in Ontario every summer. Getting back into the truck, Evelyn takes my loon with its long delicate bill protectively into the cab with her, as if it were a child that I couldn't quite be trusted with.

We leave the Cross house and drive out along the south arm of the cove, the houses between the road and the shore becoming smaller and less kempt, the yards full of nets, lobster pots, old Cape Island boats with wrinkled paint. As we pass a low weathered-shingle building with cords of firewood along the side and smoke rising from the chimney, a shout comes through the open door and my companions in the bed of the truck repeat the cry until Gilbert stops and backs up. Out the door of the building comes a scarecrow figure in work clothes, swearing imperiously and moving his arms about as if he had forgotten they were attached. He is followed by two companions who stand a few feet astern, smiling coyly at each other and us. The leader is wearing a green cap, a zippered jacket and pants of green workcloth. His frame is bent at the shoulders in the stoop of a laborer. His face, cadaver grey under the two-day beard, is long, with a pointed chin and watchful, sunken eyes. The grey pallor that merges into the rest of his unwashed skin, the disintegrating cigarette hanging from his lip, the generally baleful air, give him the look of a bogey created to scare small children. "Where the guhdamn . . . hell you think . . . you're goin'?" is his greeting.

"Well, hello there," David replies, his pleasure clear in having flushed this Caliban.

The drunk launches into a second blurry greeting full of "hell's" and "guhdamn's" but the words are half-drowned inside his mouth and he keeps losing his attention in midsentence. It dawns on me that this figure is the same "fierce old fellow" they had talked about, sitting on the lawn at Gilbert's, the one David had encountered on his visit last year. I begin to wonder if time moves at all on Tancook, if this fellow has been sitting by his smoky fire for a year waiting to pick up the conversation.

His two companions have edged closer, smiling at everyone. The rotund one is nattily decked out in a yellow short-sleeved shirt, grey suspenders and a brimmed hat of the kind that used to be called "porkpie." Under this lid a round face, round eyeholes, round cheeks. A full moon in August. Only the smile is asymmetrical, most of the upper teeth on the right side are missing. The third member is more thoughtful looking. He wears a yellow and black Pittsburgh Pirates baseball cap, a blue teeshirt and glasses. He has a small, blond, British-officer mustache, and as he removes his cigarette from his lips I see a long tattoo, blurred with age, on his right arm.

I am quietly making notes of these details when the leader notices this and, with an accuracy he has not shown before, points a long finger at me. "He's writing down! Dammit to hell! He's writing down with his guhdamn . . . uh . . . pencil!" I am an unlikely policeman but since even his two companions are looking grim, I make a show of putting down my pen and notebook, but at the same time reach down and slip on the tape recorder.

It is, in fact, David who does the interrogating, leading the drunk carefully with a series of questions to recall his, David's, name; that he took up the trade of his grandfather, the boatbuilder; that they had met on this same spot a year ago, news that is greeted by the drunk with confusion, followed by skepticism.

David then leads him through last year's conversation:

"How old do you think I am?"

Reply inaudible but profane.

"How old are you?"

"Seventy-two."

"And how old would you guess I am?"

"You're not a day over . . . over. . . ."

"I'm seventy-six years old this last April."

Disbelief. "To hell you are."

"Born over t'hill, fourth of April, nineteen seven."

A certain recognition lights the drunk's face, and a certain pleasure, as if he'd remembered his part. "To hell you are!" he says with new conviction and points at me, "*He's* guhdamn seventy-six." Laughter from the truck and from his cronies.

The drunk is right; David looks considerably less than his seventy-six years. But the surprising thing is the youthfulness of his voice. The sentences are crisp, quick, amused — none of the old codger drawls and inflections. It is the voice of a man in his thirties. Surprising too is his tolerance, his rather formally proffered friendship with this roadside drunk, given David's passionate disapproval of drinking. Most of his stories about unpleasant or negative behavior end with the line, "Well, you know, he'd been hoisting a few," or "Of course, he was drunk." Watching him perched there at the end of the truck in his spruce new jacket, an amused urbanity in his replies and questions, it is almost as if he were the mayor of Tancook, if Tancook has a mayor, or a member of Parliament, important after years in Ottawa, back home to visit his constituents. I watch David with fascination. This is not the old turnip farmer of Second Peninsula.

We finally wave the drinking party away and continue down the road. My revealing that I had the tape recorder on draws another burst of laughter in the truck bed and a story from David about a lady who recorded conversations with an old island resident. When she played the tape back he listened for a moment and said, "That sounds like a damn Tancooker!"

In another half mile the road simply ends, turning into two stony ruts going up a rise to an abandoned house. Gilbert backs the truck around and we bump back and down the way we came, giving a shout like school kids as we pass the drunks' door. At the junction where the ghost appeared we take the other road back to the harbor, passing rows of little buildings buried in the ground — cabbage houses, I am told — just their peaked roofs showing, covered with seagrass for insulation. The remarkable economy of this life.

In a barn right on the shoulder of the road, a large center door has been rolled back, and we look in at a group of five or six women handling short bunches of vegetation, other bundles hanging from the rafters, as in a tobacco barn. "Getting the savory ready," someone says. We are driving by at a good twenty miles per hour but the rich, desiccated aroma hangs in a cloud over the road, penetrating and snapping me back, as smells will do more vividly than sights or sounds, to another place: walking along the quay at Baltimore harbor with the exotic country smells rolling across the traffic from the eight floors of the McCormick Spice Company warehouse across the street. Here on Tancook, we are at the other end of the spice chain.

We return to the harbor. Topping a small rise where the thickest congregation of houses is, we start down the eastern arm of the island's road when Gilbert pulls to the side and stops. To our left, one corner nearly touching the road, is the two-story, flat-roofed house where David was born. It looks like a large shoebox, completely unadorned except for the bright blue of the shingles and clean, white one-by-four trim on the windows, which are spaced as regularly as factory windows along its side and end. The small front yard, which contains a single bush, is separated from the road by a low, chain-link fence set on a concrete base. There are two front doors, one for the original half, one for the addition that Randolph built later.

David points to the near corner of the house. The perspective seems off, the corner somehow sharpened, almost like the prow of a ship. "When my dad built the addition, this end of the house, he of course wanted to come out so far and make it square. But that ran over the line of his uncle's pasture land, over this side. Well, his uncle *refused* to sell him enough land — only a few feet — so he could make the house square. Just refused. So Dad went on and built the house anyway. That's why this corner comes to a point. It's three feet shorter on the back end."

"I think that's terrible," Francine says with a laugh.

"Isn't that something? Wouldn't sell him three feet of land. But he built it anyway." I think of Harold's memory of arriving on Second Peninsula as a boy: there was so much land, young gaffers could run anywhere. Later, talking of his thirteen tax bills and the many parcels of land he has accumulated, David says, "I think the way Dad was treated on Tancook, by his uncle, I think that stuck into me, and I was *determined* that I was going to have enough land that my children, and my grandchildren, would never have to build a crooked house."

Little Tancook is in the distance a mile and a half away as we proceed down the road, the high shoulder of the island to our right, to the left below us scattered farmhouses in their bright colors, the land flattening out in a fertile shelf for about a quarter of a mile to the shore. The road curves along the channel between Big and Little Tancook and again peters out in a grassy track. We have travelled the entire highway system; nothing beyond this but island.

On the way back, Francine prepares me for one of the high points of the tour. The owner of the farmhouse with the fake-brick siding to the right below the road has built his privy unprivily where his driveway meets the road. The story is that he waves to passers-by as he sits there, but there is no one home today.

As we climb up on the shoulder of the hill again and the expanse of Mahone Bay opens before us, suddenly the Chester Race is spread out there, full blown, a tableau stretching to the horizon. There must be more than a hundred boats, counting the various clusters of sails in the distance beyond Star Island. The vanguard, marching down the shore past us toward Little Tancook on the bottom leg of the triangular course, are the larger sloops, thirty-five to forty-five feet. They recall Peter Brown's "monstrous toys" with their striped spinnakers ruffed out in a ghosting breeze like the plumage of some seabirds of paradise. The sails seem frozen in the air, the breeze just enough to blow them up to shape, and even though we are proceeding down the road in the other direction at a good clip, the long line of boats seems hardly to move. It is an astounding sight, all that color filling the hazy emptiness of the bay so abruptly, so silently — overlapping stripes of red, black, green, ochre, magenta, gold, cerise. And for an additional bizarre touch, we are observing this parade with its tropical, designed-in-California colors looking past the garish blues, yellows, pinks and salmons of the Tancook houses, a whole other palette, a whole other culture. The sight has the surrealism of a naive painting, and the literalness as well — Tancook at one end of the bay, Chester at the other, they have been holding this parade for most of a century.

Back past the crooked house and nearly to the harbor again, we turn up a road that is bare volcanic rock for a few yards, then a track through former cabbage fields, heading across the center of the island to the Reef Woman's house. As we enter the only extensive wood I have seen on Tancook, mostly of long-needled pine, the track becomes a genuine axle-breaker. Gilbert knows the deepest holes and sharpest rocks, and proceeds at about four miles an hour with those of us in the back ducking branches and holding onto the sides of the truck to avoid being thrown from the bed.

We emerge from the wood, after an extended downhill crawl, into a landscape that is purely Canadian. When Glenn Gould titled his first radio program for the CBC *The Idea of North*, he was referring to a fascination so many Canadians have with the empty expanses of their barren and vast country. For fifteen hundred miles above the populated fringe along the U.S. border the land becomes progressively wilder, more arctic, leading eventually to the frozen seas and the icecap. Along the two coasts, in British Columbia and the Maritimes, the ocean becomes the wilderness expanse. Either way—empty land or empty sea—vistas like the one before us are what many Canadians visualize when they think of their country.

We are at the far side of the island, at the top of a meadow of grass that is moving in waves in a freshening wind from the sea. The meadow, hedged on either side by pine wood, slopes and spreads several hundred yards to the shore, out of sight below its curve. We can see the reef, a finger of broken rocks extending out from the shore, bursts of white water here and there along it as the chop breaks. A grassy island, half a mile directly in front, provides the middle distance; beyond that is ocean. Except for the roof of the Reef Woman's cottage down the hill, the scene is completely devoid of any of the marks of civilization, a scene for lovers of the north country—empty, just this side of desolate.

Our truckload of visitors bumps on down the ruts and turns in beside a decommissioned Volkswagon Beetle embedded, in true Tancook fashion, in the tall grass outside the fenced-in lawn. Its convertible top has been stove in; some tires are missing; but it has been painted bright yellow and decorated with quick, Matisse-style flowers. Beyond it are a split-rail fence, a trimmed lawn, and everywhere neat beds of Nova Scotia blooms giving off that special intensity, almost tactile, of bright colors on a cloudy day. The house is a fisherman's cottage, one-and-a-half stories, with weathered shingles and the characteristically plain island trim, painted dark red. Flagstones set in sand lead to the front door, past a fat rain barrel and a profusion of flowers planted in window boxes. The place is immaculate and tasteful. I almost expect to see a basketball hoop on the garage peak, a Mercedes in the drive, an exclusive girls' school under the trees next door.

The Reef Woman turns out to be a small, tanned-to-leather Englishwoman named Joyce Galloway, who greets us enthusiastically at the door as if she received eight visitors in a pickup truck every day at this hour. Gilbert, towering over her at six foot plus, is clearly in awe. At lunch he had described her labors restoring the house, putting on a new roof, shingling, replastering, cutting out rotten floor stringers, putting in new ones, then new floors. "It was a wreck, and she did it all by herself—amazing!" He held his hand out at chest height. "And she's a tiny little thing! You won't believe it when you see her."

I do believe it. Joyce Galloway is all energy and intelligence, with that educated English voice that ranges easily over two octaves and conveys an absolute sense of who one is, where one is—and what one expects. She wears jeans and a plaid sport shirt, her blond hair pulled back in a practical ponytail.

We are ushered into the kitchen and the exchange of news begins. On a table by the window is a copy of *Architectural Digest*, and several pages of a letter, written with the heavy nib of a fountain pen, that our arrival interrupted. Someone mentions the board hung by the front door on which is painted "The Reef Woman," and laughing, she tells how she got the name. "I was down swimming one day and two little boys came along the shore. I could see them looking at me slant-wise, trying not to be too obvious, and one nudged the other and said, 'That's the reef woman.' I liked it so I put up the sign. And that's what I've been ever since."

The conversation goes on at a brisk trot; news is shared about mutual friends; some family branches are explored, the talk mostly between Joyce, Evelyn, Gilbert and Francine. David is noticeably silent. While he clearly regards Joyce with respect—they are, despite her unrestrained Englishness, much alike—I imagine that plastering walls and replacing roof joists are skills he is more comfortable with in a man than a woman. But I expect the problem is familiar to Joyce, judging from another story, related with much amusement by Gilbert, of her encounter with the island's stonemason. She engaged him at the beginning of the reconstruction to repair the foundations and chimney of the cottage. At that point the roof was gaping and the house uninhabitable, so she and the stonemason camped out in tents, in the rain, Joyce preparing food over a campfire. He, an old Tancooker, would call down from the top of the chimney, "Get my lunch, woman," and she had to remind herself that it would not be easy to get another stone-mason to the far shore of the island to camp out in this weather. Independent but practical, she got the lunch.

I am interested in the house and leave the conversation in the kitchen to explore the other rooms. Off the kitchen is a tiny reading room with a miniature desk. Beyond is the largest room of the house, a full fourteen feet square, the living room, or more properly the parlor, for it looks as if it is rarely lived in. There is red flowered wallpaper and wainscoting to the bottoms of the windows. The furniture, Joyce tells me as she joins me from the kitchen, she has found around the country-side — delicate, Shaker-plain, early-nineteenth-century pieces, few and carefully placed. The copy of *Architectural Digest* was no whim. The wallpaper in the bathroom is a pattern from Old Sturbridge Village. Up a steep set of stairs between the parlor and the kitchen is the half-story sleeping area under the sharp angles of the roof — two bedrooms, divided at the center where the chimney rises. They too are spare, with light coming from a single window at each end of the house. In one a cast iron bedstead, in the other a spool bed set against the side wall, where the roof comes down almost to touch it — perfect for children to curl up in and become invisible. We go downstairs again and through the other rooms to rejoin the group in the kitchen. I am struck by how spare and immaculate everything is. Some people living alone leave no trace.

The eight of us make our complicated goodbyes and pile into the truck for the ride back to the harbor and Gilbert's house. At the top of the meadow I look back over the perfect, empty landscape. Joyce, I am told, spends the winter in Chester but is here during the warm months. The idea is enormously appealing and romantic images crowd my mind — the voice of Yeats, "But you shall hear wind cry and water cry, and curlew cry, and have the peace I longed for." I know also that, for a city person, that kind of isolation is its own test of the soul, takes more will than cutting out rotten floor stringers or contending with the shibboleths of old Tancook.

While we were touring the island, Goldie and her children have washed up dinner for eleven from the pump. Those dishes have been put away and the tables in the dining room relaid for tea and the cake we didn't get to before. It is a cheerful, relaxed meal as we talk over and relate for Goldie our adventures of the afternoon and I begin to feel part of the family. It is more than just sharing stories of the Reef Woman or the caucus of drunks on the backalong—we seem to be participating in a quiet annual ritual of David revisiting his birthplace. Although he can see Tancook from his own back windows, and can sail to her with a southwest wind in less than an hour, I doubt that he lands here and travels these roads and disused fields more than once a year, to see Gilbert and other family members. And it would be done this way, just a ride around the island, looking, reestablishing landmarks, commenting like an off-hand tour guide, stopping for a chat with the locals—his land, even the drunks his people.

The ferry, which we can see looking down from the dining room windows, is blowing its horn, warning of departure. It is the last boat of the day so we hurry our goodbyes and get into the pickup truck for one last jolting ride down the hill. As the boat pulls out around the concrete jetty, the afternoon sun has come partially through the clouds and the Slauenwhite house at the top of the hill is picked out against a dark sky, the reddish sun turning it a muddy orange. Gilbert and Goldie stand beside the house at the line of lawn chairs and kitchen chairs. We wave and wave again until the boat is past the breakwall and headed off toward Little Tancook. Our view swings toward Chester and the scattered retreating sails of the smaller boats, the "tailenders" on the final leg of the race course.

I find myself at the rail with "Black Bart" Shea, recently nicknamed for the thick black and grey beard he has grown. Tall, broad-chested, comfortable as a bear, Bart works as a

The *Comet,* a replica of a schooner Stevens' grandfather built in 1910.

The shop behind his home on Second Peninsula where David Stevens built most of his seventy boats.

David Stevens in his shop, carving a half-model.

David Stevens hauling the completed *Evelyn* to sea.

A gathering of the Stevens' clan for the launching of the *Evelyn*.

The *Kathi Anne II* under sail.

The *Margaret Anne* in Lunenburg Harbor.

Schooner races on the La Have River.

ERIC HAYES PHOTO

Schooners racing in Shelburne Harbor.

David Stevens and his son, Murray, with trophies won during the schooner races in Shelburne.

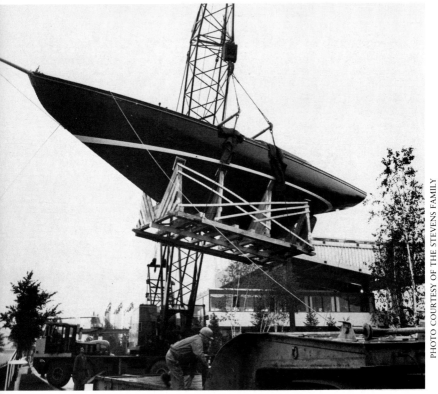

More than a million people watched David Stevens build the schooner *Atlantica* during Montreal's Expo '67. Here the nearly completed boat is being moved to the water for final fitting.

David Stevens meeting Queen Elizabeth II during Montreal's Expo '67.

The young David Stevens on Lake Ontario in 1932.

David Stevens at home with his wife, Evelyn.

David Stevens with his granddaughter, Kathi Anne, and great granddaughter, Eve. In the background is the schooner, *Kathi Anne II.*

maintenance manager at the Michelin plant in Bridgewater, half-an-hour beyond Lunenburg, but his true profession for the last twenty years has been sailing. The fact that David recruits him as navigator and first mate when the *Kathi Anne* races testifies to the level of his skill. He and Francine sailed during the schooner races in Shelburne the previous month and Bart's most severe test came on Monday, during the first race. "One of the navigator's jobs is to know the course, and I thought I had it pretty well etched in my brain. Then when we passed the second mark and came about and headed off across the bay toward Adamant West, I noticed that the two boats ahead of us hadn't come about. They were heading straight out the bay. David kept sending me down to check the course and I kept reporting that Adamant West was next. I don't know that he quite believed me. Then the three boats following us took off after the first two. That's a *strange* feeling, no matter how certain you are, when you're sailing in one direction, toward empty water, and the whole fleet's sailing in the other."

Francine, who kept the official log, later showed me her entries for this part of the race, "*Sebim* and *Margaret Anne* not heading for red stake. *Slightly* worried, 25 course checks. Skipper still questioning, eyes black. Worried navigator starting to babble. *Amasonia* and *Hebridee* not going for mark — Skipper's questions more intent — 'Mark' Shea holds firm."

"I was pretty sure we were right," Bart laughs. "How many times can you check a course? Well, it turns out we were. We won the race and the Oland Tray and five boats were disqualified."

Bart explains to me the workings of the Loran C, the radio navigation device they took with them to Shelburne but didn't use, and then talks about ocean sailing. He has made two trips to Bermuda, nine hundred miles across the open ocean from Halifax, on a forty-two-foot sloop. "I thought I might be really afraid, and the first time out of sight of land I was a little uneasy. But I got to love it out there. There's a strange peacefulness with nothing in the world but the deck and the waves."

By day they used all the usual navigational tools, but at night he found himself setting course by the North Star as sailors have since boats first left land below the horizon. As we talk, and I work out the experience in my mind, I come to another of those moments of beginning understanding, this time of the arcane business of celestial navigation. Of course. Simple. Seated in the stern of the boat, the mast is a pointer into the night sky. Day or night, the helmsman is constantly glancing up at the peak, checking for luffing, making sure he is catching the wind full. It is an habitual, recurring action, like that of a driver glancing at the car's speedometer. A course like the Bermuda-Halifax run would be almost directly north. Each time he glanced at the peak, the North Star would be there, close to the pointer. It would be a natural action to ease the helm to bring the mast or some other point in the rigging back into the right conjunction with the polestar. As David said, simple; these people couldn't read or write.

I sit on a bench on the upper deck, watching the slightly ruffled surface of Mahone Bay slide by, and think about Tancook, past and future. The future of the island is clear from the boat loads of visitors that arrive each summer day, although I doubt that many of them will gentrify its plain old houses with the skill and taste of Joyce Galloway or the familial devotion of Gilbert and Goldie Slauenwhite. Seeing the past, I have seen the reasons that Randolph Stevens took his brood and left the island in 1919. Randolph's crooked house could well stand for all the problems of people living together in small communities. It seems a kind of classic confrontation, the stingy uncle on one side, intransigent, drawing his line, waving the deed and daring the world to step over — on the other, Randolph Stevens, independent, resourceful, ambitious, building the house aslant, with that precise Canadian realism — aesthetics and uncles be damned. Neither backed down. But living in a community like that takes its toll, and although the battle between them contains the elements of age-old comedy, when David tells the story he does not see it as amusing — his voice is fresh with injustice. It is a story of poverty. When there is that little land or anything else to go around, life comes down to a matter of inches.

The other figure out of the past is the old drunk at the backalong, an acolyte of the demon rum if there ever was one. Alcoholism was the cancer of the nineteenth century, the disease that would take you down the lubricated road to hell, or at least to the graveyard, if you did not live cleanly and righteously. It was feared in the superstitious way that cancer is feared today, and living on an island like Tancook would be living in a high-risk area. Alcohol tolerance takes time to build, and a northern island, with its heavy labor during the short summers and its isolation and idleness in the long winter days and nights would provide the ideal conditions. David's father and grandfather kept occupied with boatbuilding but many others must have found little productive to do once the cabbages were stored away in their sunken houses and the boats pulled up into the fields for winter. There must have been long days and many groups like the three we met at the backalong, sitting bored by their smoky fires, waiting for warm weather, waiting for someone to come along the road through the fog.

"Oh yes, there was some bad families on the island," David recalls. "Very bad. They'd get drunk and yell and screech and brawl all over. Quite a few on the island."

Given the intensity of his feeling, I wonder if alcoholism had touched his family, and he replies with characteristic bluntness, "My mother's father was a drunkard. Spent most of the money he had on it, and my mother was deprived of many, many things because of it. I certainly remember that in my upbringing. And of course on Tancook at that time, if you heard of any woman taking a drink of liquor, she was. . . ," he searches for a proper word, "down."

I ask David if he has ever tasted alcohol and he tells of walking from Lunenburg one winter day when he was very young, stopping at a neighbor's to get warm and share a bite of food, and being tricked into taking a drink. "The fellow went down in the cellar and brought up what looked to me like syrup. I said, is it intoxicating? Oh no, they said, just like syrup." When his head began to spin from what must have been a fairly powerful home brew, he excused himself and continued his journey across the frozen inlet to Second Peninsula. "My feet just barely touched the ice. Yes," he says with rueful authority, "I know the feeling."

Recently David was nominated for the Saidye Bronfman Award, a national award given annually to Canada's outstanding craftsman. His family and friends were understandably proud because the award had always gone to artists in the usual craft fields — pottery, weaving, jewelry-making. It was the first time a boatbuilder had been nominated. A few were tickled as well because David was not aware, at first, of the origins of the fifteen thousand dollars prize money.

"I only learned after I was nominated that the Saidye Bronfman people were liquor people, Seagram's whiskey. Well, fifteen thousand or fifteen million, I didn't want their whiskey money."

"Fortunately," one of his friends says, "he didn't win."

It is easy for David's friends in the succeeding two generations to regard his absolute teetotalism as quaint — *Ten Nights in a Barroom*, come down to us from the nineteenth century along with Sunday visiting, canning and nature poetry. We no longer live on islands. We have so many ways of getting out of our houses, out of our skins — cars, television, sports, arts. The off-island life is less isolated, more complex. It is difficult to recall a hermetic life like that on Tancook, where alcohol was a sin in the old sense, a tangible danger as destructive to a small community as smallpox or adultery.

I look back along the rail at the low profile of Tancook, a warm loaf of an island in the late afternoon sun that has dropped below the clouds — a beautiful place to visit, but fifty years ago already a tight little society that was dead-ending. Randolph Stevens sensed this and escaped to the broad fields and greater opportunities of Second Peninsula. David uses the same word when asked how he began building boats: "I was born on an island. The only means of escape was a boat."

David and Bart are standing by the rail pointing to a single sail off the starboard bow. We are approaching Chester Harbor through the collection of shaved, nearly treeless islands that protect it. The race is over. Off to port we can see a few of the tailenders drifting in toward the moorings, their sails vertical and limp, cocktails, I imagine, already mixed, the level of talk rising. But the boat Bart is pointing at is off by itself—a green hull with a white deck, she still has a good patch of breeze bowing out her red, white and blue spinnaker. She appears perky and fresh and ready for a race.

"Isn't that one of your S-boats, David?" Bart asks.

"Yes," he says casually, "I believe it is."

All sails hung and slim as a dancer, the S-boat looks a fraction of her thirty-eight years. We wave as the heavy ferry plows by and receive answering waves and a distant but clear voice through the bass drumming of the engines, "Hello-oo, David!"

# SCHOONER
# RACES

$M$*onday.*   "We're going to confuse you a bit. We're going
to do it backwards. Start at the bottom of Course Number One
and read up."

The voice barely penetrates the high wind of greetings,
conversations and pre-race excitement in the public room of
the La Have River Yacht Club. The room is full to the door-
ways with schooner owners, sailors and well-wishers. All the
aluminum-legged chairs around the formica tables are occupied, mostly with people taking notes in pocket notebooks or
on the two photocopied pages of the course handout. Others,
skippers and their crew members, stand in groups to either
side, arms folded, facing the head table where the race officials
sit. All ages are here; the skippers seem to be mostly in their
fifties and sixties, the crews in their teens, twenties, and thirties. There are a few beards; young mustaches are common;
the skippers, with the exception of the mustachioed Ralph
Tingley, are clean shaven. Everyone is talking.

Behind us the bar, an enclosed counter partitioned off from the open room, is doing a steady business in six-packs to take on board. The kitchen, next to the bar, will be open in half an hour. At the moment the remains of breakfast, prepared each morning by one or another of the competing boat crews, are being cleared away. Due tomorrow morning are *Sebim*'s famous fishcakes; *Kathi Anne*'s pancakes, under the direction of Peter Peill, will be the fare on Friday morning.

When I made plans to attend the skippers' meeting before the first race I assumed it would be a cloistered affair of old salts pouring over charts and talking tides in clouds of pipe smoke, a ritual for the initiated in some inner sanctum of schooner racing on the Atlantic coast. This skippers' meeting is more like a lodge picnic moved indoors on a rainy day. Even Ralph Tingley, the extroverted secretary of the Nova Scotia Schooner Association, is having a hard time making himself heard above the cheerful conversations of people who haven't seen each other since the opening races of the season, or in some cases, since Schooner Race Week a year ago at Shelburne.

"Course Number One on your sheet," Ralph yells. "Read from bottom to top and reverse all the ports and starboards."

The choice of Shelburne last year was an exception. The schooner races were moved there, seventy-five miles down the coast, to take part in the two-hundredth anniversary of the landing of the United Empire Loyalists, Tory expatriates from the American colonies, in 1783. This summer they are back on home ground in the Lunenburg area, where Schooner Race Week is held alternately at the Lunenburg Yacht Club on Mahone Bay, at Hubbards farther to the east where the Schooner Association was founded in 1961, or to the west of Lunenburg on the broad lower reaches of the La Have River.

Through the windows that line the front wall of the clubhouse I can see the La Have River beyond the grassy patch in front of the club and through the thicket of masts and rigging of the schooners tied up, along with a few sloops and ketches, at the floating docks. The surface of the water, ruffled by a light wind, alternately sparkles in patches and goes dull in the broken sunshine of Monday morning.

I look down at the course sheet and follow it as Ralph reads.

"Bull Rock — leave it to port, not starboard. La Have Fairway — leave it to starboard. French Rock can — that's a red can way up on the south side of the channel between East Spectacle and Mosher Island — leave to starboard."

Sitting to my right at the formica table, Bart Shea makes notes as Ralph goes up the list. He is no longer the "Black Bart" of the previous summer, having shaved off his rough, pepper-and-salt beard, retaining only a full, black brush of a mustache. He looks younger and, dressed in a striped jersey, white shorts and a blue and white baseball cap, jauntier.

Ralph explains that the starting line is between the two orange buoys offshore from the club, beyond where the *Kathi Anne* is moored. Then he creates confusion by saying that the actual starting line runs from the yardarm at the side of the clubhouse, where the club ensign and pennants are flapping in the desultory wind, to the outer buoy. A series of questions follow over which is the actual starting line, an important point since most sailors plan their strategy from the ten-minute gun to reach the line precisely on the starting gun. Finally another member at the head table explains that the starting line is the line between the yardarm and the outer buoy, but boats must cross it while sailing between the two buoys. "There are two ways of looking at it," he says, and this seems to satisfy.

A youngster goes out through the screen door in front, and a large grey-and-white sheepdog scrambles into the room and dashes happily among legs. Ralph goes down the roster of evening activities for the week. Tuesday is amateur night — all crews present a skit or a song. Wednesday they will have films and slides of the Shelburne races. Thursday is a lay day, unless the Americans show up, in which case there will be an International Race. The word is that two schooners are on their way from Mystic, Connecticut, home base of the American Schooner Association, but no one has seen them, nor is anyone much concerned. There seems to be an assumption that the Americans, bested four times by *Kathi Anne* and three times by *Sebim* in the last decade, are unlikely to show up to try for their first victory against the Nova Scotians. I ask Bart where Murray Stevens is — David's son was to bring the *Margaret Anne* down from Halifax to race. He says the seas were so rough yesterday outside Halifax harbor that Murray had turned back. The *Kathi Anne*, coming just twenty-five miles around the coast from Second Peninsula on Saturday, had a rough passage of it. Many of her crew were seasick.

"Does anyone have a watch?" Ralph calls, and discussion ensues to find a watch to back up the official race clock, a large, white-faced, electrical wall clock that has been pinned to the yardarm outside and fed with a household extension cord. Power failures are not unknown. "Who keeps radio time?" Ralph asks, and a hand goes up.

"Do you have a second hand?"

The clubhouse room is all windows on the river side and on the two ends of the building, with natural wood planking covering what wall there is. In the back corner, on the land side and beyond the bar, is a lounge area with an old sofa, some upholstered chairs broken to comfort and an upright piano. The ceiling is open to the underside of the roof. I turn and look at the crowd, which has the cheerful, homogenous look of any weekend congregation at a school or a shopping mall. Here and there a few individuals stand out: a lady in her seventies, white coiffed hair, silver-rimmed glasses, a librarian's starched blouse with a bow at the neck, sits at a table by the window, the registration records and money box before her. Two young men lounge with the innocent arrogance of the handsome at a back table, dressed in polo shirts and short shorts out of the Land's End catalog. They alone in the room fit my expectations of the yachting set. David Stevens stands with a group at the side. He is dressed in a plaid, long-sleeved shirt, suntans and heavy-soled brown oxford shoes, and is talking animatedly.

"We have a few people here who want to crew," Ralph calls

over the conversation. "Who can take someone?" A few hands are raised and the unattached quickly adopted. Ralph announces the starting time for noon — it is now just after eleven — and people begin rising from the tables.

"What are we racing for today?" David calls over the increasing noise.

"The Oland Tray," someone calls back from the head of the room, "and the Cooley Mugs."

The other crews, carrying their kit bags and six-packs, file down the steps to the two floating docks where their boats are tied. The *Kathi Anne* alone is moored at a buoy fifty yards offshore. Five of us pile carefully into a leaky, flat-bottom skiff and prop our feet above the sloshing water in the bottom as we are rowed out by Eddie Peill, at eighteen the youngest of Dorothy Peill's four sons who make up the core crew of the *Kathi Anne*. A stiff breeze has sprung up and the oars thump against the tholepins as Eddie works to keep the overloaded skiff headed out toward the mooring. Before us, the *Kathi Anne* waits quietly, her turquoise hull bright and fresh against the metal-colored water.

The cockpit, where I will spend most of my time to stay out of the way of the crew, is eight feet long and four wide at the aft end where the small ship's wheel, a circle about twenty inches in diameter with six spokes, is mounted. The cockpit widens slightly at the forward end, as the beam of the hull increases, and ends at the cabin hatchway that goes down a four-step ladder to the below-decks. Set in the floor of the cockpit and centered on the wheel is the binnacle, a grey metal post with a bulbous head containing the marine compass, the only sizeable metal fixture on the *Kathi Anne*, which is otherwise all wood, canvas, Dacron and paint. The binnacle looks like a slightly dated robot. The floor of the cockpit is eighteen inches, the length of a chair leg, below the deck, which serves as a comfortable seat, backed by the low gutter board that usually keeps the spray on deck from running down and soaking our buttocks.

The blond decks, the carefully coiled lines, the neatly rolled and wrapped sails, give the twelve-year-old *Kathi Anne* an almost unused look. On succeeding days, I get a chance to inspect the decks of some of the other schooners. Each has a lived-in look, a tangle of particular lines and a cockpit full of prized equipment reflecting its owner's concerns for location, comfort or speed. The *Kathi Anne* is pristine by comparison; she is nothing but boat.

When the crew and passengers are all ferried out, there are eleven of us. Bart works away, adjusting the tension on the mainmast shrouds, metal cables that descend from the peak of the mast to deadeyes about a yard above the gunwales on either side. The tension, on contemporary boats simply adjusted by a metal turnbuckle, is controlled by a Dacron line laced back and forth through the holes of two deadeyes, one at the end of the cable, one a yard below attached to the hull. Bart pulls a line tight and refastens it with two half-hitches, then winds the remaining tail of rope down the length of the tie, for neatness.

At the foremast shrouds, Peter Peill and his cousin, Rob Peill, are doing the same. Peter, whom I met one morning last summer in David's cow pasture, is twenty-four and the eldest of Dorothy Peill's sons. He wears white shorts and is barechested at the moment, but the rolled red bandana around his head and his mustache with the ends slightly turned down, together with the habitual frown with which he concentrates on his work, give him an air that is vaguely oriental and piratical. Rob Peill, slim, with brownish blond hair and a straighter mustache, is the son of Jurgen Peill's brother, also a farmer in the Annapolis Valley. Although technically a cousin, he is clearly one of the family and a long-time crew member. Peter and Rob both resemble David, and perhaps have consciously modeled themselves on him. Quiet and intense, they go about their business with a seriousness that makes them seem a bit unapproachable, but engaged in conversation, they talk easily about enthusiasms they have, until then, kept hidden. Like David, private but not unfriendly.

On the deck between the two masts, John Rowsell and

young David Stevens are removing the fisherman's staysail from its bag and laying it out in preparation. John Rowsell is the husband of Kathi Anne, for whom the boat is named. They are new parents of a four-month-old daughter, and this is John's day to sail and Kathi Anne's to babysit. "Young" David Stevens is Murray's son, slim in Levi's and a long-sleeved jersey, with a close crop of curly red hair and the seemingly obligatory mustache. David Two, as I dub him for clarity in my notes, is one of the more experienced sailors, having spent two summers crewing on *Bluenose II* on voyages along the Atlantic coast. His grandfather, who carefully monitors the progress of each of his family crew toward the day when they might take the helm of the *Kathi Anne*, gives him high marks.

Working at the backstays on the stern deck along with Eddie Peill is a small, wiry man with white hair and beard. He is Ben Verbugh, a model-builder for the Ontario Science Center in Toronto, who drives down every year, twenty hours nonstop, to spend Schooner Race Week crewing for Murray. He and David Two are lending themselves out until the *Margaret Anne* arrives.

Francine Shea has disappeared below decks with her tub of Colonel Sanders fried chicken and numerous other bags and cartons. Although a skilled sailor who crews in many races along the South Shore, she recognizes an immutable law on board the *Kathi Anne* — women do not crew — and assigns herself to the galley, whence her knowledge of racing enables her to appear with chicken, pizza, coffee or huge cookies at just the right moments after stress in a race. Like many women in Nova Scotia she accepts the status quo with good humor and without a trace of obsequiousness. "I usually flunk on *Kathi Anne* — what else could I do with six big strapping guys on board," she writes me later that fall, and in a passage about local politics, adds her straightforward aversion to making an issue of her sex, "Every time I hear 'Women's Issues — Women's Rights, etc.' I want to throw up. I think these ghettoize women even more than if basic issues (economics, etc.) were their main concern." Philosophy aside, the balance factor in these races is clearly her respect for both skipper and boat: "Dave is so *good*, and the *Kathi Anne* such a beautiful boat to sail that winning a race is sure to come your way."

The crew numbers eight, with Francine as flunky, and two passengers, the other besides myself a calm, pretty, college-age girl named Elizabeth Haysom, whose mother is an artist in Lunenburg, and whose mid-Atlantic accent I find puzzling until I learn that she was born in Zimbabwe and grew up in Luxemburg and England before coming to Nova Scotia six years ago. She is, she tells me, busy on a novel that her agent wants before she enters college in January.

David appears from the cabin with a pair of shoes in his hand and sits on the edge of the cockpit. He carefully unties his heavy, brown street shoes and slips on docksiders. "Well," he says, taking the street shoes below, "I think we'll get under way."

Francine calls out to Ben, who is securing lines in the stern of the boat, "The pro from Toronto! Look at that, tying fancy knots in her!"

Other schooners are motoring out from the dock area, their crews standing over booms or hoisting mainsails as they go.

"Ready on the main," David says in his calm voice, raised only a fraction above conversational level. Bart and Peter haul at the lines for the main throat and peak; the gaff starts to rise nearly horizontally, peak a bit before throat; and the pristine Dacron mainsail, temporarily crinkled like an overly starched shirt, begins to unfold. A gust of wind strikes, and the sail whips and cracks against its lines like a terrified cat in a bag. "You're on the wrong side of the topping lift," David calls, and they lower the gaff several feet and maneuver the peak around a line, then haul away. The sail rises to its full quadrilateral shape. The thrashings smooth out to a more regular beat as it swings into the wind, the snapping sound deepening to a rumble as the wind plays on both sides of the tympanum. Rob and John Rowsell raise the foresail and again, not as loud this time, there is the dry rumble of the Dacron.

"Slack your peak," David calls to them.

Bart and Peter are tying off the lines on belaying pins set in a pinrail that circles the base of the mast. They make quick figure eights over the top and bottom of the pin and then, to my surprise—I would have fastened with a half hitch—simply coil the end of the rope and hang it loose over the pin. I ask David why they don't tie off the lines—each will be subjected to hundreds of pounds of weight and wind pull—aren't they afraid one could come loose? No, he tells me, the friction of the figure eight will hold, and with a loose coil if you get in trouble you can free the line in an instant—without a hitch.

The La Have River is about a half-mile across to the east shore, which is backed by low, wooded hills, the shore road dotted with white houses and every mile or two a white church. Half-a-mile below us Miller Head juts out from our shore, cutting off the view downstream. Upstream, there is clear water for several miles, comfortable room for the eight other schooners to set their sails. Some are under sail already, others still motoring along with their mainsails flapping, their crews busy at the lines.

David has sent Ben up to the bow with the dinghy to tie it off and untie the *Kathi Anne*. Bart gives the order to cast off at the same moment David says, slightly louder than usual, to David Two in the bow, "Up with the jib."

David spins the wheel as the tall right triangle of the jib fills and the bowsprit swings slowly downwind. The mainsail and foresail cease their flapping and bend out as the boat, the fifty-five-foot masts, the deck, the wind harp of shrouds and lines, all lean slowly, gracefully twenty degrees to leeward, and we hear the low hiss of white sound as the bow cuts through the water. The sensation of speed is instantaneous. Boatbuilders speak of that moment when the sails are first hoisted on the maiden voyage, first stretch out to their full length and cup the wind, as the moment when the boat comes alive. That birth is repeated every time a boat goes out—that moment of transformation when it ceases to be eight tons of wood, lead, sails and lines and is, in a silent instant, running perpendicular to the wind, a winged horse all flex and motion in a world no longer root, trunk and branch. It is probably that moment more than any other that makes pleasure sailors and keeps them coming back to the water.

"Nineteen minutes, Skip," Bart says.

We are reaching upstream, along the western shore of the river. Out in the center several boats have come about and are sailing parallel to us, a hundred yards downwind, as if following David's lead, as if he has some secret pattern in mind in the pre-race jockeying for position. The sky is blue now, the water reflecting the blue or brassy with fragments of sun, but there are high hazy patches that promise a day of alternate sun and shadow. David falls off a bit, bringing the boat more downwind and toward the center of the river. *Sorceress*, a small blue-hulled schooner with a marconi mainsail, crosses close under our stern, her deck active with crew hoisting her fisherman's staysail, her sails blocks of solid white that turn abruptly translucent as she passes between us and the sun.

"I think we'll come about now," David says conversationally, and then a moment later, no louder, "Hard alee." He turns the wheel, and the *Kathi Anne* swings as smartly as a sloop into the wind, her sails thundering briefly and then filling again as the booms swing above our heads to the other side. The crew members sitting along the deck watch them go without moving. Only Ben, assigned to the backstays, scampers across the afterdeck, loosening the starboard stay to give the main boom room, then tightening the port in quick, fluid motions.

"Twelve minutes," Bart says.

We are heading straight down the middle of the river, Miller Head to starboard, the long, straight stretch down to the village of La Have obscured by a line of fog two miles distant, lying on the surface of the water. We pass the *Maid of Uist*, which David designed and built in 1950, just after he built his first schooner for Miss McCormick. The *Maid of Uist* is a double-ender, a classic Tancook whaler of the type his grandfather, Amos Stevens, built and perfected before he turned his hand to the new, transom-sterned yachts. Her bow and stern rise up like the ends of a dory, and she has an outside rudder, attached to the stern piece and maneuvered by an eight-foot tiller. Her white hull, with a blue stripe along the gunwale, is "beamy," broad in the center, and she sits high in the water, looking heavy and slow, which she is, compared to the small, sleek schooners that surround her. She is owned and skippered by Dave Waterbury, Commodore of the Schooner Association and perhaps the most respected man for sportsmanship on the coast, for he has been coming in last, or nearly last, for years in the *Maid of Uist*, and yet approaches every new racing season with the enthusiasm of a novice. The Waterbury panache is indicated by the long, Chinese-red pennant that flies from one of the mainstays and the little black cannon on the starboard deck with which he salutes other tailenders crossing the finish line.

"Hard alee," David mumbles, and as we turn back upstream the ten-minute gun is clearly heard, a percussive shotgun blast carried downwind from the club in the stiff breeze. All nine schooners are under sail, spread out evenly across the half-mile-by-two-mile rectangle of the river, moving up and down-stream, turning about each other in a lively minuet that seems at the same time both aimless and choreographed. On board each is a man with a wristwatch or stopwatch, counting down; on board each, the skipper calculates distance, wind speed and boat speed to arrive at the starting line on the precise second of the next gun.

*Sebim* goes by with a huge-looking staysail spread along her port deck ready to hoist. All of *Sebim*'s sails look huge to me, and her batteries of stainless steel winches flash in the sunlight. David gives her a brief glance and turns his attention upriver as *Sebim* parades downstream like a shiny gladiator, the largest and most impressive boat on the river, the scratch boat, the one to beat. She was commissioned by Warren Doane, a sailor from Barrington Passage, a hundred miles down the coast, and built by David's cousin Ben Heisler in 1974. According to

David, she was designed specifically to beat the *Kathi Anne*, already at that time the winner of two international trophies, and that seems somehow to offend his sense of sportsmanship. "She's four feet longer at the waterline and carries more sail than we do," is his usual description of *Sebim* and sometimes, when he is in a bad humor, he will go on to say that her dimensions exceed the association limits, that she is not quite legitimate.

Whether the rivalry was planned or developed out of circumstance, *Sebim* and *Kathi Anne* have become perennial contenders, for ten years placing first and second in a large number of the races during Schooner Race Week. Looking over the association's records, I find that *Kathi Anne* has a slight lead in victories, but *Sebim* has come on strongly in recent years. Last year at Shelburne, *Kathi Anne* won two races to *Sebim*'s one, but the last time they met on the La Have River, two years ago, *Sebim* won four times to *Kathi Anne*'s single victory. This year, Warren Doane has retired from racing, and *Sebim* has a new owner and crew. She is now berthed at Bridgewater, up the river, and her caretaker and first mate, Starret "Sonny" Nauss, who has been working on her all winter, has been trading boasts with Bart about the speed she will show in her first outing.

"Fairly light breeze," Bart says looking glumly at the windward shore. "Better day for *Sebim* than us."

"Give me a little foresail," David says, and Eddie adjusts one of the lines running back along the cabin top to the cockpit.

"Five minutes."

I look back downriver. Three boats are working close to the starting line; most of the others are midway between us and the line. One of the four nearly identical blue-hulled, marconi-rigged schooners passes us, moving rapidly downstream.

"Which one is that?" I ask Bart. "I can't tell them apart."

"*Amasonia*," he replies, "Wes Caslake. Look out for him." He explains that the marconi-rigged boats are smaller but point well (sail close to the wind) and have the advantage of a large handicap. And Caslake, especially, is a respected skipper.

"Four minutes," Bart says, "I wouldn't get too far away, David." We are now the farthest boat upstream.

"I think we'll sail the race backward," David says mildly, "up to Bridgewater and back."

"Three and a half minutes."

"Hard alee," David says, and finally we turn and head down toward the starting line.

Eddie points across the river where one of the marconi schooners is wrestling with a staysail that is flapping and twisting in the wind. Something looks strange about it. David glances over briefly, "Have they got the staysail upside down?"

"Three minutes."

Off our starboard bow, *Sebim*'s large staysail goes up like a flag and she heads in for the center of the line. Peter and David Two take our staysail out of its bag again and begin attaching lines to its corners. David continues a course toward the yacht club, across *Sebim*'s stern. The starting line is forty degrees to our left.

Bart says, "Two minutes exactly." His voice has a pushed note to it: he wants David to turn and contest with *Sebim* for the line.

After a moment David says, "Where are we now?"

"One and a half," Bart says, then, as calmly as he can, "do you want to go for the stake now?"

David does not answer, but continues to watch the yacht club coming up ahead. To his left, the other eight schooners converge from all points on the line as if drawn by current into a flume.

"One minute, fifteen seconds."

"OK. Put up the staysail. John, give me some sheet." The foresail line is played out a few feet as David turns the *Kathi Anne* to port and points at the center of the line between the two orange buoys and toward the pack of boats converging there.

"Fifty-three seconds."

"Up the staysail."

Peter and David Two haul briskly on lines as John and Rob feed out the points of the staysail. All eight boats are ahead of us. The lead boat veers off upwind, as if suddenly changing its mind, and heads for shore. "That's what you get when you're too early on line," David says calmly, and there is a moment's pause while everyone watches the cluster of boats dashing toward the line that is invisible but, by now, as tangible in all our minds as a tape stretched across the water.

"Zero!" Bart calls, looking up from his wrist. Simultaneously the thump of the starting gun comes across the water like a tap on the side of the head. I look forward at the eight schooners clearing the starting line, their sets of parallel sails leaning identically to the left on close reaches, steering for the waters off Miller Head a third of a mile away. We are last across the line.

The day before, in a lively, long conversation with Dorothy Peill, I had asked about her father's sense of competition, and received what had seemed at the time overly pious answers. "To Daddy it's the way a race is held, the way you conduct yourself that's the important thing. He's just as happy when he loses." Her quick laughter bubbles up to contradict her. "Well, I wouldn't say *just* as happy, but he certainly never indicates that he's a sour loser. Those rules, the rules of the road that he got from his own father, who was a great sailor and a well-respected man on the water; they sail . . . they sail as sportsmen. And the thing with Daddy, in most races he always allows everybody to go across the line before he does." She reacts to my skeptical look. "Most times, if he can arrange it at all. It's sort of a . . . gentleman's way. Isn't that true, Michael?" She turns to her third son, who is passing through the room. ". . . that when you race with Granddaddy, he's always the last boat over the line?"

Michael looks a bit hesitant, searching his memory, "Well, not always."

"But most of the time."

"Yes, most of the time."

Dorothy turns to me with another chuckle, "And then usually, of course, he's out past them before too long. But he always holds back. I've been on race after race, and he's always held back and let everyone go and then tried to go out through them. All these little things, you know, make him a bit special."

"But he must be very competitive," I insist, "to have done all the things he's done."

"He is. But it's always the rules of the gentleman that govern what he does," she says in a voice that, despite her good nature, carries a note of instruction. "The code of honor. And the same with passing a boat. He will never take a man's wind. I don't think any sailor can say that they've ever seen him do anything dishonorable at the wheel of a boat just to win. Just to win a race, I don't think, is that much of a challenge, but the races he talks about are the ones where, you know, he was doing all the things he felt were honorable, and then suddenly the wind came and hit him first and he was off. I think he really *believes* that if you follow the code, things do somehow happen. And that's what makes it special."

"And you believe that too?"

She settles the lesson with her easy laugh, "I guess I believe that too."

David, when I ask him about crossing the line last, says simply that he wants to keep clear of the other boats, avoid an accident in the often pell-mell rush at the starting line. This is the explanation I would expect, the realist's explanation, but as this day goes on I will see Dorothy's romantic version realized again and again until, looking back on that relaxed Sunday afternoon conversation, I find her remarks assuming a kind of prophetic accuracy. She has called this race exactly.

In a handicapped race, among boats of different sizes, the first quarter-mile is the only part that is sailed as a unit, all the boats bunched together, the crews within conversation distance from deck to deck. It is the only part with the compressed sense of contest of a footrace or an automobile race. After that, wind and space dilute the pack, and competition is measured by boat lengths, then by minutes and quarter-miles, until one ends by squinting across the glare of the water to keep track of what is happening to the other boats. As we clear the line and advance on the pack, *Sebim*, on the land side, is forging to the front and pointing close in for Miller Head. Also on our starboard side are two of the blue-hulled marconis, *Amasonia*, with the redoubtable Caslake, and *Hebridee II*, with Ed Murphy as skipper. To port are the third and fourth marconis, *Sorceress* and *Orion*, a smaller schooner, *Elsie L*, and the decked-out, anachronistic *Maid of Uist*. Dead ahead as we advance is *Adare*, the pretty, black-hulled schooner that is the oldest boat in the fleet, the first international champion, with the ebullient Ralph Tingley at the helm.

Smoothly and without any particular sense of speed, *Kathi Anne* pulls up on *Adare* and passes her to windward. As we do, she falls briefly in our windshadow, her sails flapping limp. Tingley, with a friendly wave, swings her across our stern, out of the "hopeless position" in the windshadow, and she joins *Hebridee* to our starboard stern. The four on the port side have chosen to stay out from land, going for the breeze toward the center of the river, and are now well astern. Ahead of us to starboard, on the land side, are *Amasonia* and, comfortably in front, *Sebim*. It seems to have been only a minute, perhaps two, but we are smoothly through the pack and moving up on the leaders.

*And then usually, of course, he's out past them before too long.*

*Sebim* has chosen to pass Miller Head close in, the shortest but the most radical course. When a point of land juts out into the water, and the wind is blowing from the land, it projects a cone-shaped dead space, its windshadow, clearly seen by the smooth surface of the water out from the point. If your objective is around the point, you have gradations of choice. The closer you round the head, the larger the dead space but the shorter the route. You gamble on coasting through. If you stay far enough out there is no loss of wind but you are sailing the long way around and getting farther downwind to boot. David takes a middle course, electing to cross the dead space about seventy yards offshore.

Almost simultaneously *Sebim*, *Amasonia* and *Kathi Anne* come to a stop, their masts tilting back to perpendicular, their sails flapping, then hanging loose, the boats ghosting forward a bit on their momentum. Behind us the staysails of *Adare* and *Hebridee* begin to flap and soon they are becalmed also. It is almost as if an official had waved a flag to interrupt the race. The *Kathi Anne*'s young crew settle down, Peter and Rob lying out full on the foredeck, to wait. Bart stands peering at the water on the shore side and at the stern of *Sebim*. David remains unmoved at the wheel, his legs crossed comfortably, leaning on his left hand on the port deck, his right arm extended to the top of the wheel, his broad middle finger resting lightly on top of a spoke, sighting along the port side of the cabin.

For the landlocked reader, who may have ports, starboards and reaches wandering around in the mind like free electrons by this point, here is a quick glossary of sailing terms.

Start with the classic story: the old sea captain every day before he went on deck would unlock the drawer of his desk, glance in for a moment and relock it. When he died, his first mate, consumed with curiosity, took his keys and opened the drawer. Inside was a small piece of paper with the words, "Starboard is right." Facing the *bow* (front end) of the boat, *starboard* is right, *port* is left.

A *tack* is the course sailed at an angle into the wind. On a starboard tack, the wind comes over the starboard or right-hand quarter of the boat and the sail is on the other, or port side. To progress to windward, since a boat cannot sail directly at the wind, it performs a series of alternate starboard and port tacks, progressing by zigs and zags, much the way a road or a switchback railroad climbs a steep mountainside.

A *reach* is a course sailing across the wind, the direction of the boat approximately ninety degrees to the wind; a *broad reach* is more than ninety degrees, a *close reach* less. If the boat is turned completely downwind, you are *running*, simply being pushed by the wind, the primordial form of sailing. *Windward* is the direction into the wind, where it is coming from; *leeward* (pronounced "loo'rd"), the direction downwind, where it is going.

*Forward* is obvious, but the reverse direction is not backward — schooners are designed to move forward all the time — but *aft*, toward the afterdeck at the *stern* (back end) of the boat.

On a *schooner* there are two masts (there can be more, but fewer becomes another kind of boat), and three essential sails. Tallest and farthest astern, usually slightly aft of the midpoint of the hull, is the *mainmast* with its large *mainsail* (usually called the "mains'l" or the "main"). The *foremast* is somewhat shorter than the mainmast and the *foresail* proportionately smaller. The *jib*, the smallest of the essential sails, has no mast; its leading edge is supported by the forestay, a guy wire from the top of the foremast to the tip of the bowsprit, and is the cutting edge into the wind. On a fully rigged schooner there are several other jibs and topsails that are flown simultaneously with these basic sails and give a large schooner like *Bluenose II* the dramatic look of a front of piled-up clouds, but the Nova Scotia Schooner Association, for these races, allows only the basic sails and the *fisherman's staysail*, a roughly rectangular sail that is suspended on lines from the tops of the two masts and rides above the foresail.

Schooners are *fore-and-aft rigged*, that is, the sails are rigged along the lines of the hull from bow to stern, and generally function close to that position except when swung out ninety degrees to run before the wind. By contrast, the sails on a *square rigger*, like the clipper ships of the nineteenth century, are rigged across the center line of the hull at ninety degrees, and usually function in that position or close to it.

Traditional schooners are *gaff rigged* — the mainsail and foresail are quadrilateral, higher or peaked at the back edge, lower at the edge attached to the mast. The sail is held in place along its bottom edge by the boom, a thick spar extending out horizontally from the bottom of the mast, and along its top edge by another spar, the *gaff*, which is hauled up the mast by lines, raising the sail with it. Some of the more modern schooners have a mainsail that is *marconi rigged*, triangular like the jib and hauled up the mainmast on a track, without the weighty gaff. Marconi rigs are lighter and can sail closer into the wind, but do not have as much sail area for the height of the mast as gaff rigs. The race we are on today is actually two races. The marconi schooners are sailing for the Cooley Mug, while we and the other "gaffers" sail for the Oland Tray.

*Sebim*'s gamble has paid off. Although still in the glassy patch of water under Miller Head, her tall sails have begun to catch the wind coming high around the point, and she leans over and starts forward, clearing the point and heading close up along the shore.

"That's the route," Bart says in a frustrated voice as we continue to sit in a pool of smooth water. The western shore from here to La Have is high, rising sharply as much as 150 feet at some points. Experienced sailors know that the wind sweeping over these hills is drawn down to the water, so that the best sailing is often right in the shadow of the hill. Bart will argue this with David today, going and coming, and on every succeeding day.

*Kathi Anne*'s sails begin to flap and the crew, in an instant, is off the deck and adjusting the lines to catch the wind as it builds.

"*Sebim* got us on that one," Bart says. "She got through. But we can take her to windward up here. Sheet in, Eddie." Eddie pulls on the sheet, the rope that adjusts the foresail. We are leaning now, and the shore begins to flow by at a regular pace; Miller Head is behind us. *Sebim* is a quarter-mile ahead, off to starboard and up against the shore, heeling so far over that her lee rail is in the water. Our wind is still moderate but getting stronger all the time. We are abreast of *Amasonia*, four boat lengths to starboard, and then ahead of her. The other boats are two hundred yards astern, just pulling out from the lee of the point. *Kathi Anne* moves along happily, like a young horse given her head on a straightaway.

"I'd point up, David," Bart says, indicating *Sebim* along the shore. "Best wind in this river is up there, under the hill."

David nods but continues his concentration down the two-mile stretch of water to the village of La Have. We can see a small ocean-going freighter tied up at the La Have wharf and David is heading down the center of the river directly for her. We are on a reach, a single course that will take us down past La Have and to the gut, the narrow channel before the river opens out into a broad bay laced with islands and, beyond them, the Atlantic Ocean. There is nothing to do but enjoy the cool wind and the slapping of small waves against the bow, or, if you are inclined, stare anxiously at *Sebim*.

The crew settles down, sitting with their backs against the top of the main cabin, or lying full out on the cabin roofs. We are closer to the eastern shore now; it slides by silently with its little beaches of boulders, its half-acre of cleared land back from the water and its gentle rise of pines beyond. White churches appear like milestones, and the houses, toy white boxes with roofs black, faded green or red, seem the symbol of Victorian self-possession, their windows staring at us impassively as we go by. There is something very private about this race. In the clubhouse there were family members and friends, and a convivial buzz as at a wedding or a funeral, but once on the water, there are no banners, no committee boat, no one following us out, none of the concocted visual excitement that I had come to associate with regattas; just the nine boats spread evenly over a mile and a half of water, plowing silently on. Occasionally on either shore road, a car will pull off on the shoulder, and a figure or two get out and stare at the water. It must seem, even to the nonsailor, more than the usual procession of sail, nine tall schooners in formation. Once I see a man's elbows go up, but am too far away to tell if he has binoculars or a camera.

*Kathi Anne*'s sails begin to flap—the dry parchment sound of Dacron—and crew members interrupt their quiet conversations, looking up.

"Don't panic," Bart says. "Sheet in the staysail, Eddie."

Then he asks Peter and Rob to tighten the foresail peak. It is to be a day of spotty winds and we have sailed into a small hole. A quarter-mile upwind, we can see the white water foaming under *Sebim*'s bow and the bright blue of her deck and cabin roof as she heels over sharply. The fact that she is right on the shore, her white sails whizzing past the verticals of the pine trees, makes her speed seem even greater.

Dark cat's paws, the ripples made by sharp gusts of wind on the surface of the water, streak toward us, and we are hit abruptly with the wind that *Sebim* has been enjoying under the hill. *Kathi Anne* leaps forward again.

"Now that's what we need," David says with satisfaction. "I didn't think we'd get there without a tack."

He is still concentrating on the hull of the freighter at La Have wharf. The crew settles down again, chatting and even laughing with the general exhale of tension as the boat plows on in the firm grip of the wind. *Kathi Anne* is so silent under sail, her hull slipping through the water with no more than a hiss, that conversations in the close cockpit or on the decks tend to be in an undertone, and the rise or fall of the crew's spirits shows only in body language or slight modulations in the timbre of the conversation. Now the tone is just perceptibly higher—a feeling that *Kathi Anne* has her wind.

A squall hits us and the boat tilts abruptly, the lee deck going a few inches underwater, the submerged deadeyes making a loud sucking noise. While the rest of us instinctively bend or half-rise toward the high side and away from the rushing water, David retains his pose at the wheel, tilting with the boat, sighting along the low side of the cabin. And as the squall passes, his figure rights again, along with the masts and sails, as if he were affixed to the deck.

*Sebim* is more than a half-mile upwind now, a small patch of white sails skimming along the western shore, while we head directly for the freighter. We seem to have the shorter course but we are on a close reach, slightly into the wind, our sails flapping a bit at the leeches, their trailing edges, as the last bit of wind spills out of them. *Sebim* will be coming slightly downwind to the freighter, again giving her the advantage of speed, but somehow we are pulling even with her and by the time the two boats converge at the freighter, we are ahead. This contradicts all I know about the physics of sail — a smaller boat working upwind cannot beat a larger boat coming downwind — but here we are at La Have wharf several boat lengths ahead.

The freighter has a white bridge and a blue hull with the words "OK Service" painted on the bow, and a patchwork of rust stains that give her the character of a working salt. *Sebim* passes close enough under the bow to touch her, heeling sharply, two of her crew lying across the cabin top, their elbows hooked over the high side to keep from sliding, but we are already past the freighter and headed for the far side of the gut.

"We got her now," Bart says happily, under his breath, but a moment later David must fall off to port. We are approaching the opening to the bay and the wind, which has been coming off the western shore, now swings down through the gut, forcing us to turn off toward the eastern shore and abandon the course that would take us directly through. "We'll have to make a short tack to get through," Bart says, and, looking back at *Sebim*, apparently well behind us, "She's upwind. She's still four, five lengths ahead."

David appears to be ignoring *Sebim*. He holds course until we seem about to run aground on the boulder beach. Then with a clear, sharp command, "Hard alee!" we come about and head for a collision point with *Sebim* in midchannel. He takes us just under her stern by a boat length and then comes about again in a sharp gust from the bay, and suddenly we are sailing even with *Sebim* but four boat lengths upwind, in the dominant position, as we both head into the bay and begin to beat up toward Bull Rock. Nice work.

*Amasonia* and *Hebridee* have come up astern, and four boats are sailing through the gut, past the gas storage tanks and piles of industrial palettes on the east shore, then past the high ground of Fort Point on the west, with its flagpole and nineteenth-century cannon. *Sebim* tacks close across our stern, and I get a quick impression of blond young people grinning. Perhaps Bart gets the same impression for he says coolly, "You want to cover him?"

"Maybe," David says, and continues on the opposite tack.

After a moment, David says, "Hard alee," and we come about on a port tack, parallel to *Sebim*, but David's delay of a few seconds has put us far enough upwind that *Sebim* will not suffer from our windshadow.

*He will never take a man's wind.*

*Sebim* comes about to a starboard tack and heads toward us. "She's got her staysail down," Bart says, and then, as we cross her bow a comfortable two boat lengths ahead, "Beautiful. We got her."

David comes about to starboard, parallel to *Sebim* again, but this time a good hundred yards upwind. Off to starboard, directly into the wind, we see the Bull Rock buoy, a little tower of laced metal about eight feet high, painted dark green. Looking downwind we see *Amasonia* and *Hebridee* half a mile away along the lee shore. Rather than beating upwind with us they have chosen to take a long reach along the shore, but now they seem stopped, almost tangled together. "What's happening over there?" "Wes is aground." "Maybe he fouled *Hebridee*." It is too far for any of us to see clearly.

David calls quickly, "Hard alee," and we swing about to the port tack, *Sebim* following our move four boat lengths behind. "I nearly missed our mark," David says, looking at the green buoy about seventy yards upwind. We are moving away, will need to go a few hundred yards out on a port tack to get high enough on the wind to swing around and make the buoy. A half-mile down on the lee shore, *Amasonia* and *Hebridee* have disentangled and are heading toward us.

David glances back at the buoy, now well astern, and comes about. We are on a starboard tack again and heading directly for the mark in a moderate breeze. As we bear down on the buoy there is the sense of relief one gets cresting a hill; we are over the hump and starting down the other side. Things ease up. Then, unexpectedly, a shiver of alertness runs through the crew and all eyes go to port.

*Sebim*, rather than following us on a starboard tack, has continued her course and is bearing down from our port quarter on a line that will meet ours right at the buoy. There is a murmur of surprise that grows to incredulity as she continues toward us. One of the oldest rules of the sea is that a boat on a port tack gives way to one on a starboard tack, but *Sebim* comes on, oblivious, toward the point of collision. "Starboard!" Bart calls across the water as she approaches, her crew members like statues on the deck; then, cupping his hands, "Starboard!" again. No answer. There is a moment of disbelief, of dream, as the sails of the two large boats tower up, blotting out the sky.

Then David spins the wheel, swinging the *Kathi Anne* up ninety degrees into the wind. Her sails flap thunderously as *Sebim* swishes by no more than a few feet from gunwale to gunwale, and tacks neatly at the buoy. We have fallen back, dead in the water.

"Overlap mark! Three boat lengths!" Bart yells. "Buoy room!" (Later he admits this was a bogus call—we had no overlap by then and could not call for buoy room—but in his frustration he was prepared to try anything.) This time *Sebim* calls back, "OK," but does not give room. In a moment it is academic; she is around the buoy and off greyhounding in the good wind. In our effort to avoid a collision, we have lost headway completely and now drift like a log down below the buoy. There is nothing for it but to repeat the maneuver, to climb laboriously up and around the buoy again. David spins the wheel, and the *Kathi Anne*, like an old lady getting up from a park bench, swings painfully back over to port and begins to pick up wind. Slowly the buoy moves down past us, and we have enough headway to come about to starboard and clear it. *Sebim* is two hundred yards ahead, trailing a festive white wake behind her as she plows along. I am furious.

So are the crew, and there is some low-grade muttering as they move about setting the lines. Francine says, "Well, we could certainly protest that one!" but David says nothing and eventually the crew members distribute themselves over the deck again and sit watching the retreating stern of *Sebim*. Half a mile beyond Bull Rock the wind drops on all of us and the boats slow to a walking pace.

David says, "Leeward side. Move over. We need some ballast," then, to Francine and others of us in the cockpit who are still rumbling and simmering over *Sebim*, "If I'd defended my rights, I'd have cut her in two." This is all he says about the incident at Bull Rock.

*It's the way a race is held, the way you conduct yourself that's the important thing.*

Our course is for the La Have Fairway buoy, halfway between Mosher Island and West Ironbound in the middle of the broad bay; it is the fair channel marker for ships coming in from the Atlantic. Both crew and wind have settled down after the excitement at the buoy and there is a pause, during which Francine passes up brown pieces of chicken from the tub in the galley. I discover I am ravenous, as are the crew members; only David refuses the food. The bay is open water, several miles in each direction, to the south opening to the ocean. On the leeward shore there are rock cliffs, the black of an old burnover mixed with red and yellow stone colors, green bushes and on top the ever-present dark green pines. On the windward side, East Spectacle Island and Mosher Island blend into one low, green line.

Bart, who is sailing his home waters, talks to David about the various windholes in the bay. "Oxner Rock, the deadest place in the bay. Wind goes straight up." He counsels him once again to stay up on the windward side.

David nods but keeps his course dead for La Have Fairway. "At least we've got steerageway. Pull in the main a little, John."

In contrast to our steady plodding straight for the marker, *Sebim* has gone off on a broader reach downwind. Now she approaches us, having gone over to a port tack, and passes slowly right under our stern, about ten yards distant.

Henry Andres, her new owner, standing at the wheel, calls across the open space, "Sorry for that buoy."

"So are we," someone calls back. There are smiles and the matter is put to rest.

After a few minutes, the wind drops almost completely and David and Bart discuss whether to come about. "Go to the lee side, some of you fellows," but even with extra weight to port, the sails just hang and flap gently in the light breeze that seems to be shifting around to our bow. *Sebim* has come about to a starboard tack, parallel to us and about a third of a mile up, and has wind. She is boiling along, her lee rail awash again, and a minute or so after her comes one of the blue marconis — it looks like *Hebridee* — also pulling out in front of us. It surprises me how the wind is in some places and not in others just a hundred yards away, how on a day like this you can find the wind and then lose it just as abruptly, as if a hand had lifted it from you.

We come about to a port tack — David wants to take advantage of the wind shift — but there is no wind and we sit. Slowly we swing back around to starboard so that we are at least pointing toward the buoy. Bart sits, his chin resting on his hands, while *Sebim* and *Hebridee*, upwind where he wanted to be, dash on toward the mark. For the third time today the race seems lost, and the crew and passengers relax and talk among themselves. I go down into the cabin for a second piece of chicken.

Coming back on deck, I look out to see if *Sebim* has made the buoy. For a moment I can't locate her, and finally I have to ask, "Is that *Sebim*?" pointing to a pile of sail way downwind toward the lee shore and half a mile below the buoy. In some mysterious way *Sebim* has slipped downwind and into a hole. Perhaps she followed a slow windshift coming more and more off the ocean, swinging her by degrees farther away from the buoy. Too late, she comes about to a port tack and starts to climb out, but she no longer has the brisk wind that took her there.

Meanwhile, in our straight-on course, we have picked up a

little speed, and it is clear that we will make the buoy before her. We are only second, however. *Hebridee* is still upwind of us and advancing down on the buoy with better speed on a broad reach. We are perhaps a hundred yards away now, and I can see the bright stripes of red and white on the marker and pick out the words "La Have Fairway." As we watch, *Hebridee* reaches the buoy, sailing across our bow, but at that moment the wind quits entirely and we are all becalmed. *Hebridee*, like a car sliding on ice, moves smoothly by the buoy, unable to turn. About fifty yards beyond she manages to bring her bow around, but has lost all headway and sits there, her sails flapping in slow motion, her crew hauling lines, while we creep slowly up on the mark. David, concentrating on the slightest breath of wind on his skin, moves her up to the buoy with the delicacy of an old person feeling for footing, and we round the mark inside the stopped *Hebridee*.

We can do little more. What headway we had is slowed by small rolling waves now coming in from the ocean. Half-turned to starboard, we drift and bob a hundred yards beyond the buoy, with *Hebridee* watching from her hole, and *Sebim* beyond her, still climbing slowly up to the mark.

When the wind returns it comes in a blow, and all three boats spring to life. *Sebim* rounds the buoy before *Hebridee*, still untangling herself and getting a hold on the wind, but we have already come about to a port tack and are well upwind and heading for the channel between Mosher and East Spectacle Islands, and there is a liveliness in the crew that suggests that, with any luck, we have the lead for good now. Bart sights up the channel and says happily, "*Sebim* is going to lose her shirt in here." And indeed there she is, on a port tack but half a mile below us and pointed down toward the lee side of the channel, while we churn briskly up to windward, our higher position giving us a good several minutes on her.

How did David manage it? Was it luck? Can he see the wind? One of his prized stories, which he tells with fresh pleasure even though twelve years and fifty other races have intervened, is of the elimination trials for his first international race in 1972. The *Kathi Anne*, barely a week old at the time, was racing against *Adare*, the little black-hulled schooner that had captured the first international two years before. *Kathi Anne* was one race down, so the second race of the two-out-of-three competition was essential to her.

"Yes it was quite something, that second race with *Adare*. At one point they were two miles ahead of us, and we thought that was it. One of my crew got so discouraged that he even went down below and sulked. But we got enough wind and caught up with her, and we started in for the next mark when the wind suddenly died out on both of us. Now when I left Middle Ledge I said to my crew, I'm going to head straight for the next buoy. And the *Adare* — the wind was southwest — the *Adare* kept up so I wouldn't get to windward of her, but I said I'm going to make a straight run for it. Well, there we were about two, three hundred feet apart, right abreast of each other and it was flat calm for ten minutes or more and we both just sat there, as helpless as could be. And *firrrst* thing [when David is in the story-telling mood, he drawls out his emphases like a character actor], I heard a great noise, and I *looooked* in the opposite direction that the wind was — and there was a gale of wind coming so it would hit me first."

"The opposite direction from *Adare*?"

"Yep, one hundred and eighty degrees from where the wind was. Never saw it happen before or since. And of course it struck us first and *awaaay* we went, and the poor *Adare*, it took a long while reaching her. And until it struck *Adare* we were probably a quarter-mile in the lead, and we finished. It was a miracle," he says with matter-of-fact conviction. "There's no question about that. No question about it in my mind. So then we had one each. And the next day we finished, I think, four or five minutes ahead of her, so that gave me the right to meet the American boat. But if it wouldn't have been for that miracle, the *Adare* would have had it that year. But it just seemed that . . . the Master of the Seas was with me."

*He was doing all the things he felt were honorable and then suddenly the wind came and hit him first and he was off. I think he really* believes *that if you follow the code, that things do somehow happen.*

In a matter of minutes the red cone of the French Rock can, near the shore of Mosher Island, appears off our port bow. It is a bit high for us, so David swings the *Kathi Anne* over to a starboard tack to get a few yards upwind and then back to port, and like a broken-field runner avoiding the last tackle, she slips around the can without breaking stride and takes off down the channel between the two islands, leaning into the strongest blow of the day. We all brace toes, hook elbows and fingers over extrusions on the deck, as the *Kathi Anne* heels at forty-five degrees reaching down the channel, leaving a white trail of foam thirty yards out the stern. The sounds of wind in the rigging and water boiling under the hull blot out conversation and we hold on and grin into the wind. Francine climbs out of the tilted cabin doorway and passes cans of Coke. David refuses with a shake of his head, then says he'll have a bit of water — his first refreshment of the day. As he sips from a plastic cup, Francine takes off the striped trainman's cap she has been wearing and puts it on David's head. "You have to have my lucky cap."

We are at the end of East Spectacle Island by the time *Sebim* and *Hebridee* have reached the French Rock can. We can look between the two Spectacles, which on the chart do look like two lenses of a pair of glasses, back into La Have Bay, where the tailenders, two miles downwind, are just making their approach to the Fairway buoy. We glide by a deserted farm on West Spectacle, the main house a weather-stripped, imposing, two-story affair with a "Lunenburg bulge," a second-story bay window in the front that rises to a small Victorian tower. The main barn has rectangular holes in the roof, while a smaller outbuilding is represented only by a collapsed roof that angles up out of the tall grass, the supporting walls gone decades ago.

Approaching the end of West Spectacle, David prepares the boat to jibe around its point; our course now will take us at a right angle back into the bay. Jibing is the reverse of coming about, swinging the stern rather than the bow across the wind, and in a high wind is a ticklish, sometimes hazardous maneuver. When the bow of a boat is swung across the wind, for a portion of that arc, thirty degrees at least, the sails lose wind and flap loosely; the boat slows; the pressure of the wind on the tackle is abruptly lifted, to pick up again gradually as the bow swings to the other side. If the stern crosses the wind, however, there is no such pause. The leech, or trailing edge of the sail, catches the wind immediately and slams the sail, boom, gaff and all, over to the other side. To reduce the force of the blow, the sails are trimmed in as much as possible before the helm is swung and let out immediately after, so the arc of the jibe is short. On the *Kathi Anne*, with a boomed jib and a staysail up, this requires every crew member on at least one set of lines.

David has everyone at their stations and now is watching the long sandy point of the end of the island. The land enters the water at a very flat angle, and he is suspicious. "How close in can we go here?" he asks Bart.

"Lots of water here," Bart replies. "Go as close as you like."

David calls "Jibe'o!" and spins the helm, and *Kathi Anne* neatly turns the corner, the mainsail swinging across over our heads with a thump that can be felt through the hull. There is a moment of frenzied activity as the crew pays out lines.

"Someone on the backstay!" David calls, and Ben leaps across the stern deck. Then we have turned directly downwind and the silence of running settles over us. Running before the wind, especially if you have just come off a brisk reach or tack, has an eerie feeling of limbo to it, as if you had somehow switched off the wind. By looking at the wake or a piece of land going by, you can tell you are still moving quickly, but since you are moving with the wind, you can't feel it on your skin, or hear its rush past your ears. The world is flowing by but the boat seems suspended in a cube of still, hot air. If the sun is out and reflecting off the great pans of the sails, you begin to bake.

The crew remains at their sets of lines, carefully trimming and adjusting as they feel what the wind is doing. Rob is standing on the foredeck, leaning on the foresail boom to keep it spread out to starboard. The *Kathi Anne* is running "wung out," a descriptive local term for carrying the mainsail and jib out on one side and the foresail, balancing them, on the other. It is the logical arrangement for a two-masted boat, so the mainsail does not shadow the foresail, but this spread-eagle position gives a schooner its fattest and least characteristic look, and a group of schooners wung out takes on the exotic appearance of a fleet of junks.

We are probably making close to seven knots, moving across the open bay in our envelope of warmth and silence. Several crew members have removed their shirts. I look back at the end of the island and see *Sebim*'s sails, translucent in the sun, moving briskly along above the meadow grass. It is an incongruous sight, reminding me of the tracked cloth targets on an army target range. The Big Shoal Conical is now visible in front and moving up on us. When I look back again, *Sebim*, *Hebridee* and *Amasonia* have rounded the point and arranged themselves in a wung-out parade pointing in our direction. As I watch they seem to grow just perceptibly larger and, in our cocoon of still air with its strange sense of stasis, I have to put down the nightmare feeling of running and remaining in place.

Rounding Big Shoal Conical we jibe again and set off on a port reach for Bull Rock, at the entrance to the river. Bart and David engage in a predictable debate on the course — Bart says point high, David not so high; but David turns the wheel over to Bart and goes below for his first break. It is four minutes after two and he has been at the wheel two and a half hours. John Rowsell breaks out a cigarette, but Francine and I, the other two habituates, refrain. Smoking is not strictly forbidden on David's boat, just mutely forbidden. The chicken bucket is passed around and with it great slabs of homemade bread. Bart talks cheerfully of his rivalry with Sonny Nauss, "When we beat him out to the gut, that was it for me. The race was over." He can foresee a long winter of happy needling.

We are approaching the mainland now, taking Bull Rock and continuing on the same port reach. The wind remains strong. *Sebim* and the others, still a quarter-mile astern, do not seem to be moving up after all. The sun has gone in and the shoreline is dusted with a low, thin fog that gives it a bluish cast. I am not yet prepared for how quickly the weather turns along this coast. Shirts go on and a nylon jacket or two. Francine, her timing perfect as ever, brings out hot coffee and auctions off the last three pieces of chicken. Peter Peill scuttles over the top of the main cabin on all fours, a chicken breast clamped in his teeth, looking more piratical than ever.

Bart cuts the *Kathi Anne* close under the blue hull of the freighter at La Have wharf and points up the two-mile stretch of river to Miller Head, and beyond it, just out of sight, the finish line. David has come back on deck and sights up the river. He and Bart argue one more time about the course, David advising the center of the river, Bart keeping the *Kathi Anne* pointed in along the high western shore. "You still don't believe me, do you?" Bart says without rancour. "You gotta keep the faith a little in this river." David does not reply, but sits and allows Bart to keep the helm.

*Sebim* is following our course, with the two smaller boats just behind her. She seems to have gained a bit on us, but although the wind has lightened, we are making good time up the shore. The thought is barely down in my note pad when there is a sharp flapping of Dacron overhead and the endlessly fickled winds of the day die again.

"Don't panic," Bart says to no one, to himself. "Just lost the wind a little." It returns a moment later, before our forward motion has slowed. The crew settles down again, sitting along the sides of the cabin, watching the green shore with its occasional farmhouse nestled under the hill and the occasional passing car on the shore road. No one looks aft, but the festive mood that took us so buoyantly from French Rock can to La Have has settled to a quiet watching. *Kathi Anne* is doing what she can, eleven minds thinking her forward. Each time I look back, *Sebim* appears fractionally larger. Francine says quietly, "This is the longest stretch of the course—to that line."

We pass a small, delicate, blue-hulled schooner, her sails

furled, riding at anchor near the western shore. David identifies her as the *Melissa Sue*, built by Jim Rhodenizer, his most-valued helper in the days of the boat business. "He's a wonderful builder," David remarks. But then, squinting at the boat riding in the shadow of the shore, says, "That mainmast seems too far forward."

The clouds have built up so that, as we approach Miller Head, both sky and water have turned grey. "Better go for the line," David says, and Bart, almost ritually now, replies, "No, better stay out. Remember this point on the way out." But he gives the helm back to David for the finish. *Sebim* is still a comfortable quarter-mile astern.

David steers close in around the point, and as the yacht club comes into view, the sails begin their familiar flapping; the masts tilt back to vertical, and once more we slow. So close to the finish line, whose orange floats we can see bobbing up ahead—is David steering into a hole? But the flapping of the sails picks up to a thunderous whipping from side to side. Instead of a hole David has found a sharp heading wind, swinging around the point and directly at us. He falls off to starboard, and *Kathi Anne* leans comfortably and is off again, with one last, relieved exhale from the crew.

"Take down the staysail," David calls. As the wind continues to build, five men haul on the lines, and the staysail comes down, thrashing and cackling like a netted bird, continuing to struggle until it is thrust by quick hands into its sack. The wind is strong and is now coming almost directly downriver at us, forcing the *Kathi Anne* to head off toward the eastern shore. Everyone is chatting again, the level of conversation rising with the wind, but we are now pointing well below the outside buoy, sailing along parallel to the finish line. A hard gust allows David to point up a bit and, satisfied with his position, he comes about to a starboard tack and heads for the center of the line.

The buoy to starboard lines up with the yardarm to port, its flags and ensigns standing out horizontal in the wind, and as they come up ninety degrees on either side, we hear the punch of the gun from shore. There is no cheering, either on board or on shore. We are alone at the finish line. David swings over to a port tack and heads briskly up the center of the river.

"Take down the foresail," he calls and, as the crew wrestles with the flapping Dacron, turns to Bart and says quietly, "Thanks, Skipper."

David Two is standing on a supporting stay alongside the bowsprit, his hand on the jib stay, grinning broadly, enjoying a ride out in front of the bow wave. As the crew rolls up the foresail and secures its Dacron ties, David, still at the wheel, turns talkative. "There's nothing to racing in a steady wind, but soft winds like today, fickle winds, that's something else. Anyway," he says, looking contentedly at the busy deck of the *Kathi Anne*, "boat-for-boat, she's good enough."

Francine remarks again on the near-collision with *Sebim* at the first marker, and David says, "We won't bother to protest them," which brings a laugh along the deck.

"Some people," Francine says with a shake of the head, "they know you won't hold."

But David reminds us that *Sebim* has a new skipper and crew. This is their first race.

"We'd better get them a port-starboard hat," someone says, drawing another laugh, "or red and green socks."

We come about and start downriver again. Rob and David Two have struck the jib, but we are still moving briskly with just the mainsail. We approach the line from the inside as *Sebim* comes upriver toward it, six and a half minutes, the record eventually shows, after our time. *Amasonia* is right behind her by twenty-five seconds. Well in the lead, boat-for-boat, for the Cooley Mug, she will lose it to *Hebridee* on corrected time.

We approach the dinghy tied to our mooring and David swings the *Kathi Anne* around 180 degrees to the mooring as if she were a small catboat. Rob reaches down and grabs the side of the dinghy, and we are home. At the same time *Sebim* crosses the line near us, and a voice calls across the water, "Congratulations! Well sailed!"

*Tuesday.* From the *Kathi Anne*'s cabin where I am storing my gear I hear the bass rumble of the mainsail going up and then a lighter, splatting sound, as last night's rain, caught in the pockets of the folded sail, showers down on the deck and the steps into the cabin, soaking those in the cockpit or below near the hatch opening. Coming up on the wet deck, the day looks no more promising—a grey carpet of clouds with blond spots here and there where the wind has rubbed it thin. The brightest sight on deck, standing out from the background of grey water and dull shoreline, is the canary yellow oilskins of the crew, heavy weather gear that is normally stored under the bunks in the cabin. Some crew members wear full suits, others just the jackets or the pants held up around the chest by broad suspenders, giving them a uniform but ragtag look, like a partially equipped guerrilla force. I find the temperature still comfortable for my light windbreaker and do not investigate the oilskins.

The crew is a version of yesterday's, less Ben who has gone to Halifax to see what happened to Murray and the *Margaret Anne*. With the addition of Mike and David Peill, the middle sons, the line-up of four Peill sons is complete, along with Rob, the cousin; John, the son-in-law; and David Stevens Two, Murray's son. The female passenger today is Stephanie Frank, a slim young woman in jeans with close-cropped brown hair, who flew in yesterday from Germany. Her father is a plant geneticist from whom Jock Peill imports many of his high-yield strains of wheat. David Peill has been interning with the Frank business in Germany, and yesterday during the first race he and Mike were at the airport to meet Stephie.

"Any time with the foresail," David says as the crew, in its bright pieces of yellow, moves about the deck. "Cast off. Up with the jib."

The *Kathi Anne* moves upstream in a brisk wind that is blowing a bit from the western shore but mainly down the river toward the starting line.

In the clubhouse this morning, the results of yesterday's race were posted on the wall next to the kitchen:

| Boat | Rig | Elapsed Time | Corrected Time | Oland Tray | Cooley Mug |
|------|-----|--------------|----------------|------------|------------|
| *Kathi Anne* | G | 2 46 27 | 2 43 26 | 1 | |
| *Sebim* | G | 2 53 05 | 2 53 05 | 2 | |
| *Amasonia* | M | 2 53 30 | 2 48 20 | | 2 |
| *Hebridee II* | M | 2 57 42 | 2 45 25 | | 1 |
| *Adare* | G | 3 12 15 | 3 02 19 | 4 | |
| *Maid of Uist* | G | 3 24 32 | 3 09 43 | 5 | |
| *Sorceress* | M | 3 27 46 | 3 07 04 | | 3 |
| *Elsie L* | G | 3 36 45 | 2 56 18 | 3 | |
| *Orion* | M | D N F | | | |

*Kathi Anne* was the clear winner of the Oland Tray for gaff-rigged boats, both on corrected time and boat-for-boat, without a handicap. The positions of the others, however, were decided by the rating sheets, now printed out on the ubiquitous greenbar computer paper, that the officials poured over in the clubhouse after the boats were tied up and the skippers and crews had mixed their first drinks.

The same nine boats are sailing today, and as they jockey for position in the mile of open water above the clubhouse, I begin, with Bart's help, to sort them out. The four marconi-rigged, blue-hulled schooners, all thirty-some feet in length, are the most difficult, but *Hebridee II*, Bart points out, has a "doghouse," a natural wood cabin that rises up four feet above the deck, giving her an old-fashioned, unstreamlined look. She is owned and sailed by Ed Murphy, who has a dry-goods business in Halifax. From any distance, *Amasonia* and *Sorceress* are nearly identical. Wes Caslake, *Amasonia*'s skipper, is a dentist who practices in Bridgewater, up the river, and lives in La Have. *Sorceress*, two feet shorter but otherwise the twin of *Amasonia*, is sailed by Joe Graves, another Halifax businessman. *Orion*—at thirty-three feet, nine inches, the smallest of the four marconis—is owned and sailed by the only woman skipper in the races, Dr. Marty Lawrence, who teaches family medicine at Dalhousie, Nova Scotia's major university, in Halifax. Her crew is all women, and while a "woman's boat" seems an anomaly in the male-oriented Nova Scotia Schooner Association, later in the week I meet Willa Creighton, a tall, confident woman with the long-distance gaze of a sailor, who skippered her boat *Airlie* in the first official race of the Schooner Association at Hubbards in 1961, and came away with the Colonial Fisheries Trophy.

After the four marconis, the identifications get easier. *Adare* is the only black-hulled schooner, and is the granddaddy of the fleet, built as a Tancook fishing schooner in 1902, five years before David Stevens was born. She was owned by the late Victor Oland, brewery magnate and lieutenant governor of the province, whose company also commissioned and built *Bluenose II*, and is now sailed by Ralph Tingley, a friend of the family. Ralph has put a lot of work into reconditioning *Adare*, and with her black hull, white cabin and bright orange decks, she has a warm-country, Mediterranean look to her.

I have no trouble picking out the antique profile of the *Maid of Uist*, now the farthest boat upstream in the pre-race maneuvering. Dave Waterbury, Bart tells me, is a lawyer in Kentville.

We go by the stern of a small, white-hulled boat with blue trim, the *Elsie L*, designed and built in Massachusetts by the American designer William Crocker. At thirty feet, she is one of the smallest boats in the fleet but Bart speaks approvingly of her: "A very nice little boat, lots of headroom." *Elsie L* is owned and sailed by Alf Lohnes, a naval architect himself, and rear commodore of the association. It is his computer that keeps the ratings.

After yesterday, I know the remaining boat in the fleet; the formidable *Sebim* sails smoothly under our stern and a call comes across the water, "Good luck, you guys." Someone on our foredeck returns the salute.

The ten-minute gun goes off, its report a distant thud in the heavy air. David looks briefly back at the line but continues his course, reaching across the river toward the eastern shore. Francine is laughing over Ralph Tingley's complaint that his young crew yesterday were all going about the decks with walkman radios and headphones. "He said 'ease the sheets' several times and no one heard him. He thought he'd have to go below, call the radio station, and ask them to announce it."

"Six minutes, Skipper."

We sail on quietly, the crew mostly sitting, looking out over the grey water. Perhaps it is the depressed weather, but things are calmer today; there is a more settled, workaday air aboard the *Kathi Anne*.

"Four minutes, thirty seconds."

We come about to starboard and David points her downstream toward the starting line on a broad reach. We are up about half a mile, the *Maid of Uist* above us, the others all working back and forth down near the line.

Approaching the windward shore, David asks, "How's the time?"

"You've got two and a half minutes," Bart replies.

"Give me a little mainsail," he swings the *Kathi Anne* more downstream as the yacht club comes up on our starboard bow. "Backstay," he calls, and Eddie moves quickly to loosen it.

"Watch the foreboom!" It swings over, and Peter puts his hand up and pushes it into position. We are approaching the line wung out, the wind at our backs.

"Watch the mainboom. Stephie, keep down a little." She has been sitting on the cabin top, where a sudden movement of the boom could catch her on the side of the head. Now she crouches on the deck as we approach the congregation of boats at the starting line.

"Staysail ready."

As the starting gun goes off, David calls, "Staysail up." At the same time he swings a bit to starboard, causing the foresail to jibe, pulls in the main sheet and we are off on a broad reach, pursuing the sterns of the other boats. Except for the *Maid of Uist*, still a hundred yards upstream, we are again last across but begin immediately advancing, downwind of the pack, and by the time we pass Miller Head (no windshadow today; the wind is coming downriver, across the point), we have taken the lead. The *Maid of Uist* is now over the starting line. The other seven boats are all upwind of us, toward the western shore, following the preferred course. *Amasonia* leads the pack, still wung out. *Sebim* gets some wind and passes *Amasonia*, who crosses her wake. *Adare* and *Hebridee* are in close pursuit. We watch this contest from the center of the river, as if it were another race. We are well in front and headed once again directly for the freighter at La Have.

A long calm settles over the cockpit and decks. David Two and David Peill, Peter and Rob sit along the starboard side, talking quietly. The rest of us are in the cockpit, shoulder to shoulder. Even Bart is quiet. He found yesterday's race frustrating—David insisted he sail as navigator, then argued with him on every course. But Bart knows himself well enough to know that much of his frustration was settling the winter's scores with his friend Sonny Nauss. That over, a clear victory under his belt, he is today much more in David's easy rhythm. But I expect he would be, victory or no. I have yet to see anyone in these Nova Scotia waters carried away by winning. Competitors they are, no doubt about that, but proudly diffident in their competition.

*Sebim* has separated herself from the pack and is coming up slowly to starboard. Once again we are in a two-boat contest. *Kathi Anne* excels working to windward in heavy weather, and the race we are in at the moment is supposed to be her poorest, running before a light wind, but even though we can hear the slosh of *Sebim*'s bow wave as she draws to within thirty yards of us, she does not seem able to close the gap.

"In on your main a bit," David says quietly as the freighter at La Have comes up. "Little bit more. In on the foresail." He is sheeting in, looking for a change of direction as the wind comes through the narrow gut from the bay.

"Fores'l all right?" Mike asks in a murmur, and David nods. The orders and replies are all in an undertone. David rarely raises his voice in any circumstances and on a quiet day, with a light following wind, his commands have the intimate quality of late-night conversation around a kitchen table. Stephie and David Peill sit with their backs to the cabin, conversing quietly in his newly-learned German. The others simply watch the shoreline, ignoring the boat following us.

"Should I pay any attention to this mark?" David asks as a stake comes up dead ahead, just off the rocky windward shore.

"You can go a boat length inside if you like," Bart replies with the same calm.

We begin to be hit by small gusts of wind coming around the point. *Sebim*, behind us, keeps turning up with each puff, trying to get to windward, but David just says, "Flukey winds," and keeps his course. We are hugging the windward shore of the gut—yesterday we had to tack across the full channel to get through here—and as the open waters of the bay begin to appear around the point, a steady wind hits us.

David says, "Boys, I think we'd better bring that fisherman down." He says it in the same level tone but there must be a note in the voice audible only to a Stevens ear, for the crew leap to their feet; their hands find lines, and in a matter of seconds the staysail, tugging in the now sharp wind, is on its way down toward the deck. They work at top speed and with maximum economy. The *Kathi Anne* is heeling at a good forty degrees, and David Two balances precariously on the low side, back against the shrouds, feet braced against the cabin, as he bags the whipping sail. In another moment the bag is stowed and the crew settled on the deck again in various poses of nonchalance. I am impressed, as I will be all week, with the anticipation that David has trained into them. There is never a moment when the right hands are not at the right point to trim a sail, execute a tack or jibe, but in between the flurries of action, explosive and complex as the plays in a football game, they sprawl on deck with the ennui of teenagers trying to think up something to do on a Saturday afternoon.

A flight of thirty cormorants crosses our bow, long-necked black birds whose rapid wingbeats keep them just a few feet above the water. On the shore to starboard more cormorants perch on boulders, their necks curved like question marks, watching the procession of white sails. We have been beating up to Bull Rock, and now David comes about to a starboard tack and we clear the mark and head out for the center of the bay and La Have Fairway.

The wind is getting cooler. Fog, as it did late yesterday, dusts the shoreline, giving it a bluish, distant look. Out in the open bay toward the marker, fog appears to lie on the water like a thin comforter on a bed. Nothing much to that—it looks as if you could poke your head through it by standing up. The sun is out, but a weak, yellow sun; the sky remains a dirty grey. Along the shore under the burnt rock cliffs are little alternating flashes of white. They are waves breaking on the shore, and seem picturesque and puny from this distance.

Bart announces that *Sebim* is one minute back as she rounds Bull Rock. He is timing us at each buoy, an action that will shortly prove important. The swells begin to reach us from the open sea, slow, oily rollers that lift and drop the little choppy waves made by the wind. At some point I realize that we have been listening to the lugubrious two-note sound of a foghorn coming downwind from the lighthouse at the point of Mosher Island. Another flight of cormorants, like an escort, skims low off our starboard bow, black arrows pointing the course.

Spray is coming over the bow, and those who were not fully uniformed take pieces of oilskins handed up by Francine from the cabin. The water runs in rivulets down the deck and trails off the stern; thanks to the gutter board against our backs, the cockpit edge where we are sitting is still dry. Through the sound of the foghorn, we hear the short, unmusical clanks of the La Have Fairway buoy. At first I am surprised—I didn't note it as a bell buoy yesterday—then remember that we had approached it in a near dead calm.

We pass the buoy, rocking and clanking in the growing swells, and David sheets in, keeping the same tack, and points up for the next mark, a buoy called False La Have, out beyond Mosher Island, at the edge of the ocean. False La Have marks a channel that could look like the river's mouth to a boat coming in from the ocean, but goes behind Mosher Island and dead-ends in a graveyard of rocks.

As the *Kathi Anne* heads close into the wind the foresail boom begins jigging up and down in its tightly hauled harness. The lighthouse on Mosher Island is clearly visible, sitting on top of a rock cliff fifty feet high. Around the base of the white column are two houses and two small worksheds, all white with red roofs and backed by dark green pines. Waves are breaking at the base of the cliff — a calendar picture. Behind us *Sebim* rounds La Have Fairway, still an even one minute back. The sea swells are larger — it seems to me a good one meter from trough to crest — and *Kathi Anne* begins to labor, crunching down into them. By now the cold has thoroughly penetrated my windbreaker, and I go below to put a sweater under it.

Francine is lying in one of the bunks, looking comfortable and unconcerned. Mike passes me, going up the steps to the deck, putting his arms through a slicker coat. I find my sweater, and my head is encased in it as we come about and the world goes off its axis. Objects slide, fall and clatter in the cabin. I rebound from the starboard bunk and, holding onto the trunk of the mainmast that bisects the cabin space, struggle into the sweater and put my jacket back on. I reach down to refasten my kit bag and find, bent over double in the dark cabin, I have trouble working the catches.

Back on deck, the world has nearly disappeared. The lighthouse and its whole cliff of rock are gone; *Sebim* is nowhere to be seen. Looking back, I catch a brief, ghostly sight of *Amasonia* rearing and plunging into the waves. Then she is absorbed behind a curtain of grey and we are alone.

"Stephie," Edward says with a note of worldliness in his voice, "this is fog."

It seems only a minute since we were sailing along within the comfortable arms of La Have Bay, but now we could be in the North Atlantic in November. We are, I am suddenly aware, pointing toward the open ocean, dependent upon finding some marker to swing us around and bring us back to land.

The waves begin to crest above us. I look out to starboard and find myself looking at their midsections. At the top of each rise, *Kathi Anne*'s bowsprit is pointing disconcertingly to where the sky would be, and as we plunge down into the troughs it comes close to going under the water. The decks and sails of the boat are still sharp and clear, and the yellow slickers of the crew blaze with color, but beyond this all is a dark limbo and I am touched by the chill of isolation that must touch all sailors who venture out beyond land and help. There are only twelve of us and we are alone.

I should say thirteen—for the first time I think of the *Kathi Anne* as a person, or at least as an animate presence, striving through the waves, carrying us on her back, and understand for the first time the full import of that easy personification with which ocean sailors refer to a boat as "she." I think too, gratefully, as she rises up and over the crests of waves with hardly a creak breaking the wind and silence, of the extra bolts and knees David put into her—"That makes a very secure job, I would say."—and the hundred thousand hammer blows that forged rivets in her hull.

David comes about to a port tack, and Bart comes to the door of the cabin. Behind him his charts and navigation tools are spread out on the table for the first time. He looks businesslike.

"How many yards offshore?"

"Maybe three hundred," David answers, referring to the world of grey in front of him. Bart drops back into the cabin, lurching awkwardly against the roll of the boat, and begins to move a parallel rule across the chart. I can't understand how he can work, head down, in that pitching cabin—I am keeping my nose to the wind for dear life.

"Speed and course!" Bart calls up from the cabin.

"About four," David says calmly. "Southwest, one-ninety."

Later, when I have recovered, Bart explains to me the principles of dead reckoning (at that point, awash in dizziness and growing nausea, I would have found even the name unsettling). On his chart, he has drawn a line like an open, backward

"Z," extending from La Have Fairway to the open water, then angling, the first tack when I was below, toward Mosher Head, then turning again out to the ocean, then a tack and a long straight line to the mark for False La Have. The angle of each line comes from the compass setting of our tack, the length from our speed and the time we are on the tack. The importance of timing each buoy and each tack becomes clear. Bart gives me the time-honored formula—distance times sixty divided by speed equals time in minutes. If the compass settings are right and he and David correctly estimated the speed of the *Kathi Anne* in this shroud of fog, we will reach False La Have in fourteen minutes.

But sitting huddled in the cockpit, watching him work over the chart with his arcane instruments, looking up at the silent grey void in which all our motion is up, down or sideways, I have no comprehension of what Bart is doing. His activities seem about as relevant as witch-doctoring. The idea of finding an eight-foot buoy in this blind vastness of the ocean seems existentially absurd, and I know in my cold-invaded bones that it will not happen. We sail on in silence.

At this point my notebook has a single, rain-splotched entry: "The next 30 mins. are sheer misery." That is probably the best description, for there is little to be said about seasickness that is adequate to the experience. It is the most misery the body can feel, short of clear pain. It is your life's largest hangover, multiplied by ten. Looking back I know it began in the cabin at the moment my head was imprisoned in the sweater. We came about; the lip crumbled beneath my feet, and I began the, at first, slow descent into the vortex, the disappearance of all the landmarks of the mind. You find yourself staring at a door latch, a foot, a piece of rope as if you had never seen one before. You look away from this and climb for the air and the horizon line, if there is one, and point your nose into the wind because somewhere down there is the promise of stability. And even as you are thinking that, full awareness and full disorientation wash over you, and you are totally adrift in a world that will never again be solid. The fog is like the whirlwind.

My condition must have begun to show, for someone hands me up a bulky, navy blue jacket from the cabin. I crawl gratefully into its protection, sweater, windbreaker and all, fumble with, then give up the zipper and sit hugging it around me as it deflects the piercing wind. Rain has begun, and my ballpoint pen refuses to take on the wet page but this does not matter. I am too weak to maneuver the pen anyway, and sit there holding the pad and pen in my lap, staring with what is left of my sight toward the plunging bow of the *Kathi Anne*. We are alone on the ocean, approaching the edge of the earth. The misery goes on for hours.

At twelve minutes, the yellow slickers begin to line the port side, listening for the clank of the buoy. We all concentrate on the anonymous fog to port and there is a suspension of talk and motion as we try to penetrate it with our eyes and ears. Staring into fog is hallucinatory. Shapes begin to boil before your eyes, and you begin to hear sounds where there is nothing but the wind and the low laboring of the hull going down into the water. There are several false hearings from one member of the crew or another, followed by a general, quick shaking of heads. We hold still again and sail on in the sound-deadening fog. Then from a great distance, but clearly, we all hear four dull clanks of metal on metal. David Peill extends an arm toward the fog wall, and the crew unfreezes and goes back to their stations. David has registered the point of sound, but turns his attention forward and sails on, his internal clock ticking, waiting for the moment it will signal the tack to port to make the buoy.

The tolerance of this right angle turn is very fine. If he tacks too soon we will pass below the buoy. Circling around and tacking back in this soup would not only lose several minutes, it would bring us into the paths of the oncoming boats groping through the fog. If he tacks too late and we are too far above the mark to windward, we might miss it altogether—sound does not travel far upwind and the clanking of the bell could be swept away from us as we sail out for Spain.

"Hard alee!" David calls, and swings the *Kathi Anne* hard to port, up and across the heavy line of waves, around and down into the trough. The main sheet plays out rapidly. Stern nearly to the wind on a broad reach, we are, for better or worse, roaring down into the fog with the speed of a power boat, searching for the lost clank of the bell. The moments of silence stretch out until it is clear that we have missed it, that it is somewhere in this muffled void a quarter-mile behind us. Then the urgent voice of David Two from the bow: "Buoy dead ahead! Dead ahead!" There, forward on a collision line, is a tall green monster of a buoy, lifted on the waves, coming at us out of the fog, the words FALSE LA HAVE looming up ominously like a warning out of *Pilgrim's Progress*.

We would have run it down but for the cry from the bow; as it is, David passes so close the tip of the main boom almost brushes it. Past the buoy David swings us completely downwind, Peter and Rob push the foresail over to starboard, and the silence of the downwind run settles over us. David posts David Two as a lookout in the bow; then he and Bart set the course and the time for the next buoy, West Ironbound, down there somewhere several miles in the fog.

The cessation of wind is a blessing—I release the jacket I have been clutching around me and find my fingers enough to fasten the zipper. At the same time the fog above our heads thins, and a cone of light, almost sunlight, covers the *Kathi Anne* and reflects off her sails. Crew members settle comfortably on the foredeck and talk begins again.

David speaks up sharply for the first time, "Keep those conversations down up there. I have to be able to hear the lookout."

The talk stops immediately, and everyone turns to the port bow. They have been reminded that these are the most hazardous minutes of the race. Looking back over this moment later, David says, "My biggest worry wasn't hitting the mark, I knew we'd make that all right, but the oncoming boats—in order to get up to the mark we had just left they had to work out across our path and I'd be coming right side onto them. If he would be coming across and I'd shoot out of the fog—you'd have to act in an instant, split second timing—or I'd ram him right amidships. Dangerous."

Silence has settled over the boat as everyone stares into the fog again, tensed for the appearance of a bowsprit or the dim white triangle of a jib. David Two stands at the bow, motionless as a figurehead. But with each minute that goes by the tension drains as we leave the area of convergence around False La Have and move into waters where we are still fog-blind but confident we are alone. Finally everyone settles back to enjoy the run as the *Kathi Anne* boils along, rising comfortably up on a heavy roller, shuddering a bit, as with pleasure, as she slides down the front side into the trough.

I sit very still, hunched in the corner of the cockpit, sunk to my chin in the voluminous, warm jacket, feeling the euphoria of a boxer who is out on his feet: I congratulate myself on being upright, and know at the same time that only absolute stillness will hold the body together.

I never do hear the bell for the West Ironbound marker. The *Kathi Anne* jibes smartly around it, the mainsail passing over our heads with a substantial *chunk*, and sets off on a brisk, broad reach in a direction that is supposed to be back into the bay and to La Have Fairway. Another ten minutes of fog blindness, and from the bow comes the ancient call, "Land ho!" which on shore might have struck me as hackneyed, but now comes with a relief that must be as old as the words themselves. In thirty seconds, in a manner that can only be described as phantasmagoric, places appear in the fog, the lighthouse and its white buildings to port, a green headland to starboard, the broad pan of La Have Bay in front of us, materializing sharp and fixed as ever. We are in bright sunlight sailing across the blue bay, La Have Fairway a mile directly ahead, the white sails shivering vigorously in the wind. It is like coming out of a dream and seeing the familiar walls of your room, realizing they have been that close all the time.

The yellow jackets and pants start to come off, the crew emerging in its cutoffs and jeans. The swells begin to die and the boat's up-and-down movement smoothes out as she cuts efficiently through the small waves of the chop. Behind us the receding bank of fog looks harmless, just a grey smudge at one point of the broad sunny bay, in the middle of which we sail alone.

Minutes go by and still no sail appears out of the grey line on the horizon. We are approaching La Have Fairway when Bart calls from the foredeck, "Hey David, are we lost?" Everyone looks to starboard, and there is general laughter as we see a large, white motorship coming up to a parallel course, with a familiar red crane on the aft deck and the words "Tancook Island Ferry" along the bow.

"I told you we'd end up in Mahone Bay on your course," David calls back, to more laughter. The ferry crew, on their way up the La Have River for repairs at a local shipyard, wave as they go by.

As we round Le Have Fairway a single sail has appeared out of the fog behind us, too distant to tell who it is, and as we come up on Bull Rock a hot wind suddenly hits us off the land. The remaining pieces of oilskin disappear, shirts come off, and the North Atlantic sailors of thirty minutes ago become sun sybarites again. It feels as if we've sailed halfway around the globe. David turns the helm over to Rob and takes his first break of the day. I gratefully return the bulky jacket to the cabin, along with my own poor windbreaker and sweater, and come on deck feeling human.

The course back up the river from the freighter at La Have wharf is directly into the wind, and we make many tacks, but it is still the suntan run, the crew members lying easily around the decks, squinting at the shore as David works the boat back and forth across the river. There are three sails behind us now, but still a mile or more distant. The wind remains brisk, and as the *Kathi Anne* heels over at forty degrees, I spend the time up along the port side, holding onto the shrouds and occasionally getting a wet foot when she leans in a stiff gust, enjoying the sense of speed that is much greater on the foredeck than in the cockpit. With your hand on a shroud you can feel the muscles of the boat working as they tighten and slacken in the gusts, and you partake to some extent of the helmsman's feel for her.

The yacht club seems deserted as we come up, but someone is still on duty, for the gun thumps as we cross the line. We are the only boat in sight, and it is a curious kind of finish, as if we had been racing the clock. John Rowsell surprises me by remarking as we cross the line, "That was the best sail of my life." I can't say the same.

Fifteen minutes later we sit comfortably tied up at the buoy and watch a racing finish, *Sebim* and *Amasonia* contesting for the line. *Sebim* crosses *Amasonia*'s bow and tacks, coming parallel to her course and the finish line, but *Amasonia*, swift little whippet, pulls even with her and is about to pass when *Sebim* begins falling down on her, forcing her away from the line, then tacks and crosses the line thirteen seconds ahead. We look on without comment. Then Bart points to a fourth sail that has rounded the point, "*Hebridee*'s the one you have to watch for — corrected time." And that proves to be the result:

### MEMORIAL TROPHY

| Boat | Elapsed Time | Corrected Time | Position |
|------|------|------|------|
| *Kathi Anne* | 3  31  42 | 3  27  37 | 1 |
| *Sebim* | 3  46  04 | 3  46  04 | 5 |
| *Amasonia* | 3  46  17 | 3  39  17 | 3 |
| *Hebridee II* | 3  49  23 | 3  32  43 | 2 |
| *Adare* | | D  N  F | |
| *Maid of Uist* | 4  40  30 | 4  20  30 | 6 |
| *Elsie L* | | D  N  F | |
| *Orion* | | D  N  F | |
| *Sorceress* | 4  13  30 | 3  45  24 | 4 |

Later still, as the last boats are coming in, David, Bart, Mort Pelham and some others stand around in the clubhouse discussing the problems of racing in fog. *Hebridee*, we learn, found False La Have by using a hand-held radar unit.

Bart, who has already been down along the floating docks where the schooners tie up, "getting the stories," reports on *Sebim*'s navigational problems: "They went out and out and out after La Have Fairway, and then tacked back in and they were at Mosher's Head. They practically went back around."

"Easy to do," someone says.

"No," David replies to a question, "I don't have radar. No, no, I have Bart Shea," and after the laughter subsides, "and I could smell the land."


*Wednesday.*   Bridgewater, eight miles up the La Have River where it narrows and a bridge can span it, has an enclosed shopping mall, the only one, to my knowledge, south of Halifax. It is built low along the river, fronting the same public wharf where, years ago, the Sadie and other Bush Island boats would dock and exchange cargos of haddock for cabbages and coal with the farmers of Lunenburg County. The interior street of the mall is paved with universal tile; the storefronts are new old-brick and have a pleasing, understated look, which, together with the soft music and the carefuly dimmed lighting, create an atmosphere that is constant and restful. The glowing plastic signs seem familiar as blossoms, and the shop interiors with their deep mazes of mirrors, cloistered gardens. The engineered weather makes me think of the natural weather off False La Have yesterday in all its raw mutability and of the youth-evoking quality of being exposed, in reasonable doses anyway, to heat, cold, rain and the unconditioned air. One experience, however, I have no nostalgia for: a long history of getting carsick, bussick, airsick, boatsick and, probably originally, cradlesick. I seek out the drugstore at the south end of the mall and head for the shelf with pills for motion sickness.

I rediscover, if I had forgotten it, that seasickness is a mental disease. As I walk down the drugstore aisle past the hundreds of bright, blurry pill boxes, bottles, plastic-bubble cards and tubes, the colors bleed; the vinyl floor begins to wave beneath my feet; and I feel the familiar, warm sweat of apprehension. A bit greenly I ask at the counter for Gravol, which they have handy right by the cash register, take the paper bag and push through the glass doors for the cool air and solidity of the parking lot, as amused at myself as I am nauseous. The mind can be a trying companion. Alone in the cabin of the *Kathi Anne*, I pour a drink from the plastic five-gallon container of water and gulp down a double dose of Gravol, which settles the horizon that day for good.

For once the weather is perfect. The far shore of the river looks closer by a quarter-mile in the freshly washed air, and squads of small puffy clouds, contrasting with the deep blue of the sky, march down from the north. Our crew and passengers number fourteen; in addition to the five Peill grandsons, two granddaughters, Margaret Anne and Mora Stevens, have joined their brother, David Two, so David is sailing with nearly the whole third generation of his family. Stephie is with us again, but John is not. The other passenger besides myself also carries a note pad and pen. She is Marilla Stephenson, a blond young woman who is a sportswriter for the Halifax *Chronicle-Herald*.

The wind is downriver, and it is a straight run to La Have, breezy, brilliant and uneventful. *Sebim*, *Amasonia* and *Kathi Anne* alternate the lead, with black-hulled *Adare* nipping at our heels. As we pass the ferry dock, Francine brings up cokes and pan pizza from the galley. I have no memory of food on yesterday's race—perhaps repression, perhaps Francine's unerring instinct for when to feed. David has a cup of water.

I think of a conversation the previous summer with David Callan, a young businessman in Lunenburg who frequently sails on the *Kathi Anne*. "If you race on other boats, the crew spends most of its time yelling at one another and running to man the winches. On the *Kathi Anne*, you get under way and David sends someone below to bring up the canapes. It's almost no fun, sailing on David's boat. There's so little to do."

The course is the same as yesterday's—after La Have Fairway, we haul in and point up for False La Have at the edge of the ocean—but it is through a different world, a world so drenched with light that even the misty rim of the ocean has lost some of its cool infinity, and those sights directly around us have a sun-warmed, miniature look—model villages and trees with green sponge leaves. A mile forward a Cape Island boat coming in from the fishing grounds trails a small blizzard of gulls. The lighthouse on Mosher Head is a brilliant column of white today, the pines behind her, vivid dark greens. At the base of the lighthouse a small helicopter sits on a patch of green lawn atop the granite cliff, as if drying its wings in the sun. We pass a hundred yards offshore and David points below *Sebim*, a few yards ahead of us, and directly at the mark.

"You don't want to duel with him a little bit, do you?" Bart asks. By the rules of racing, the downwind boat has the right-of-way and, as we draw even, we could force her up, away from the mark.

"No," says David, "just want to sail my own race." It is one of his favorite expressions.

We are about a mile off Halibut Head on Cape La Have Island and approaching False La Have, yesterday's lost mark looking obvious and unmysterious in the light of midday. We prepare to jibe around the mark; the crew members go to their assigned sets of lines and David sends the passengers and the women below. Francine, Margaret Anne, Marilla Stephenson and I troop down the hatch steps and stand around the trunk of the mainmast in the narrow cabin, observing what we can out of the hatchway and the cabin windows.

After a moment, I hear David's voice from the helm, not loud but unmistakable, "Mora, go below." The younger of Murray's daughters, the seventeen-year-old Mora, has not joined us in the cabin. Through the hatchway I can see the edge of her figure—she is standing motionless against the aft end of the cabin; her arms on the cabin top would be at the set of lines for the foresail.

"Mora, go below," David says a second time, taking more attention than he wants from the approaching jibe. Mora's figure remains at attention at the foresail lines. She crews on her father's boat and she is determined not to be herded into the hold like livestock on this one. Finally David cannot insist; the buoy is here.

"Jibe'o!" he calls, and the tackle swings over our heads, thumping and ratcheting with additional resonance in the hollow sound box of the cabin.

"East by north is your course," Bart calls, and as Marilla and I come back on deck the crew, including Mora, are busy tying off lines at their new settings, a broad port reach across the open end of the bay toward West Ironbound Island, two and a half miles away. *Sebim* is ahead of us by seventy-five yards and seems to be pulling away.

David calls down into the cabin where Francine and Anne have remained talking, "You can come up now, girls."

To which Francine calls back, "Can I take my chain off the stove, Dave?"

No one else talks to David this way but there is something about Francine's cheekiness that he enjoys, and will answer back smartly in kind or, as in this case, in silence. (In another few years, I suspect, he will get the same pleasure from Mora, now defiantly tying off the foresheet with her back to him.)

"Now comes the test," David says to no one in particular, "windward work."

I am sitting on the low side as we swing around the West Ironbound mark. The boat heels sharply as we pull into the wind; my back drops toward the water. The decks and cabin tops rise well into the sky. Along this horizon of gunwale comes the red ironwork and light of the buoy, rearing up eight feet above my head, so close I think I could stand up and touch it, and I anticipate the scrape of the hull that does not come. David is too slick for that; a boat that touches a buoy is disqualified.

We have hauled in to a close port tack and pointed up as much as possible toward La Have Fairway, but will have to tack to make it. In fact, we are at the farthest downwind point on the course, the bottom of the windhill, and it is all up from here back to the finish line. This is what David is counting on.

*Sebim* is off to leeward, about a quarter-mile ahead but down-wind; she does not seem to point as high as we do and is headed more toward Gaff Point and beyond it the burnt rock shore. To starboard is the picturesque saddle of West Iron-bound Island, invisible yesterday, its farmhouse and barn cra-dled in the middle of sloping fields that rise to a high dirt headland at the north end, identified on the navigation charts as "Conspic. Bank."

We take down the staysail, which complains as usual until forced into its bag—"More nuisance than it's worth," David remarks—and settle down for some serious windward work.

Another three boats have rounded West Ironbound; *Adare* leads them, but begins falling off immediately toward the shore, unable to point up with the younger, lighter marconis.

Bart eyes *Sebim* off to leeward and says to David, "Don't want to tack yet, do you?"

"Not yet," David replies. He hunches over the wheel like Rumplestiltskin, staring ahead calmly, without expression. *Sebim* comes about to starboard, crossing our bow about a hun-dred yards ahead. Bart again suggests coming about, but David continues on toward the eastern shore, away from *Sebim*. When he finally does come about, pointing out across the bay toward the lighthouse on Mosher Head, *Sebim* comes about to port, the two boats sailing toward each other, and crosses our bow again a hundred yards out.

We are now in a perfect crisscrossing pattern with *Sebim*. Our courses, overlaid on the chart, would make a series of squat diamonds, and my normal sense of leader and follower is lost, *Sebim* and *Kathi Anne* either moving toward each other or moving away. Only at the moment of crossing do we dis-cover how the race is going. The next two times we pass, things seem about the same; about a hundred yards separate us.

We make the La Have Fairway marker and continue the same tacking pattern toward Bull Rock. Coming up from get-ting a sweater in the cabin, I see the marconis about half a mile astern on our tack, *Adare* far astern and laboring into the wind along the rock cliffs. We converge with *Sebim* and this time she passes us a little closer, maybe six boat lengths. David seems to be watching the scenery. I know his internal clock is going, metering the wind direction and speed, the wave height, his memory of tides and the current from the approaching river mouth, but none of this is revealed as he brings *Kathi Anne* about, as if to keep time with *Sebim*, across the bay from us, and the crew routinely roll over the cabin tops to the windward deck. This time *Sebim* crosses us by three boat lengths, and although we swing out on another starboard tack that seems identical to the last six and *Sebim* seems to be performing exactly the same as before over by the rocky lee shore, the next time we converge we cross her by 150 yards.

Francine looks at David, a touch of awe in her voice, "We picked up three minutes on that last tack."

"That's what you call cutting them down," he grins and his eyes sparkle with a stronger blue than they reflect on land. "If you can hold it."

"Gramma should be happy now," Michael remarks. Of all the trophies to be won this week Evelyn Stevens wants a year's possession of the MacAskill Portrait, an old framed portrait of schooners, similar to the photograph of the *Bluenose* race in Halifax harbor that hangs above the sideboard in their dining room. She had instructed her husband to bring it home.

"Oh not yet," David replies to Michael, "long way home."

But we have crossed *Sebim* twice more and she is now a half-mile or more astern as we come up on the green buoy at Bull Rock, which goes dark in the shadow of our sail. "Just leave a coat of paint," Marilla says under her breath as we brush by the marker and head up for the gut, conversations rising along the deck with the sense of homing.

Again it is a long chain of tacks up the river but the wind is brisk, the sky, although thoroughly tufted with sheep clouds, remains a resolute blue, and *Kathi Anne* forges ahead on her favorite point of sail, windward into a stiff breeze, leaving the other boats a fixed half-mile downwind. We are in the clear center of the river heading toward the low eastern shore, when

I ask David if I may take the helm of the *Kathi Anne*, just for a moment, to get the feel of her. He regards me without enthusiasm but is too polite to refuse and moves one place down in the cockpit, allowing me to sit close and grasp the wheel. It is like grasping the air. There is no pull, no pressure on my hand. Cautiously — David is watching me as if I were trying out my first bicycle — I move the wheel some degrees clockwise, and, slowly, in an airy, lazy way, as if she had heard the request from a distance, the *Kathi Anne* swings a few degrees to port, then settles comfortably on her new setting. I take my hand off the wheel and it stays.

"The schooner rig," Peter Brown tells me, "is the most perfectly balanced of all sailing rigs. That's why they developed as fishing boats — they could almost take care of themselves while the men hauled nets. If the masts are just perfectly placed, as they are on *Bluenose II* or *Kathi Anne*, the boat will be fingertip steering — less than fingertip steering." He proceeds to tell me the story of *Kathi Anne*'s first race with *Agamemnon*, which struck me the first time I heard it as a tall story, but which, upon each repetition acquires more detail, more corroboration, until I must view it, as it is viewed on the South Shore, as the stuff of legend.

The year was 1974, and *Kathi Anne*, the winner in international competition the two previous years, was facing the winner of the Great Schooner Race at Gloucester, the *Agamemnon* out of Miami and Nassau. Among the crew of thirteen, mostly the usual collection of children and grandchildren, was Harry Bruce, the newspaper columnist. After describing the comfortable lead that *Kathi Anne* established in the first race, Bruce wrote, "Then, a beautiful thing happens. Stevens announces that *Kathi Anne II* has slipped into a groove in which she is so finely balanced she will sail herself. We go below and when the committee boat pulls near, the race officials see a fully-rigged schooner, with her sails perfectly set, flying over the Atlantic ocean with no crew."

"It was absolutely fantastic," Dorothy Peill says, recounting her version of the race. "We were off in Mahone Bay; the committee boat was coming up, and the man on the committee boat, he'd always been bugging Daddy — calling him before the races — well, don't take any women on board or you're going to lose; lower your boom; do this, do that; telling Daddy how he should win. And of course Daddy, you know, sort of sloughs those things off, like a fly off your shoulder. But he's got a good enough sense of humor that he couldn't resist making a point with this guy. So the committee boat was coming astern about a quarter of a mile and so the whole crew went down below. We pointed the *Kathi Anne* and down below we watched the compass in the cabin, and with nobody at her helm, she inched higher into the wind."

"You didn't lash the wheel or anything?"

"No, never! Just left her. *And she steered herself closer to the wind than any human hand could do it.* And we sailed along for about ten or fifteen minutes and she never waivered. She never waivered from that compass point. And then we passed a buoy and had to tack, so Daddy crawled back into the cockpit on his back and put the helm over — and Murray crawled up and sort of loosened one backstay and tightened the other — and they crawled back down again. I think we were down there twenty or twenty-five minutes, and the committee boat — Daddy peeked out the cabin window and they had their binoculars trained on us — they couldn't believe their eyes, this ghost ship going along." She laughs with fresh delight, then more seriously, "But it was . . . really phenomenal. That's the sign of true balance. I think once in a million you find the perfectly balanced boat. *Bluenose* had it. And *Kathi Anne*."

David has only one point to add to the story, "I met the fellow — the fellow with the binoculars — on the street in Lunenburg the following week. 'What did you think of the race?' I asked him. 'Which race was that?' he says, all cautious. 'The one on Tuesday.' 'Oh,' he says as if he'd just remembered, 'It was very good.' And that was all he had to say. Never a mention. But I didn't get much advice from him after that."

As we pass Miller Head we come up on the smaller boats that have been sailing a shorter course for the Admiral Pullen

Trophy. We parallel the *Maid of Uist* for a bit, coming across river on a starboard tack. The *Elsie L* is about fifty yards behind and downwind. David runs past the line, right into the harbor and nearly to our mooring before coming about and heading back to the line and the finishing gun.

"Well that makes three," he says without expression as we head upriver and the sails begin to come down. Another, louder explosion makes us all jump and we look over to see a cloud of white smoke blowing out from under the red banner of the *Maid of Uist*. She is second in the Pullen race by twenty minutes, so is announcing her own arrival. As we watch, the scarecrow figure of Dave Waterbury scrambles up to the foredeck to reload the cannon in time to salute *Elsie L*.

*Friday.*   Thursday was a lay day. Since no American appeared to challenge for the International Trophy, there were no formal races. Most of the boats took part in what Marilla Stephenson described in her article in the *Chronicle-Herald* as "novelty races," a single-handed race and a race in which the boats sailed downriver for an hour, then turned and sailed back, creating a natural handicap. David was not racing so I spent the day in Halifax, in the editing rooms of the National Film Board's Atlantic Studios, running and rerunning Kent Nason's rushes of the planking of the *Evelyn*. David took the opportunity to escort his great-granddaughter to the Bridgewater agricultural fair, officially the 93rd South Shore Exhibition, that had begun the day before. "I need someone to take me on the merry-go-round," he deadpanned. "My granddaughters got too old for that sort of thing, so I had to wait until the next generation came along."

Friday morning I go down to R. B. Stevens and Company, Ltd., the sail loft at the end of Second Peninsula, to meet Harold Stevens. We sit in kitchen chairs in the middle of the varnished loft floor while Harold recalls, with warming pleasure, the days when he and David were boys and newly arrived from the rocky fields of Tancook. I stay longer than I intend and it is approaching eleven o'clock as I drive down the west side of the river from Bridgewater to the yacht club. I'm still in reasonable time, since the *Kathi Anne*'s crew doesn't start ferrying out until around eleven-fifteen, so I am surprised, rounding the point above the club, to see the river full of sail. As I come down the driveway to the parking lot, the shotgun thumps, starting the race. Today's is the longest race of the week, Mort Pelham tells me, standing on the front lawn of the yacht club—twelve miles down to Indian Island Light, beyond False La Have, and twelve back—so they moved the starting time up to eleven. He thinks there is still time for me to get on board and summons a young man, who takes me in an outboard to where the *Kathi Anne* and the other boats are drifting beyond the starting line—it is a uniformly grey day with a dead-looking sky and not the slightest ripple on the water—but David waves us off. The race has begun and his mind is on wind, or the lack of it, not disorganized passengers. I wave and wish them luck—now I know what missing the boat means—and we head back for shore.

It will be good to get another perspective on the races. Back in the car, I drive down past the procession of sail to the ferry dock at La Have and pull into the parking lot with several other cars to watch the sail-past, or what is today more accurately the creep-past. *Sebim* is first, as usual, in what is a kind of slow-motion progression over a sheet of grey glass. The second boat is new and easily spotted, even though she is well over toward the eastern shore half a mile distant. She has a "bright" hull, the only one in the fleet, and hanging above her trio of standard white sails, her staysail is a solid red, giving her a flag that could identify her ten miles out. I have seen her only once before, hauled up in the shop in winter, but I have no trouble recognizing the sleek, clipper-bowed, natural wood *Margaret Anne*. Murray has arrived from Halifax.

*Amasonia* comes along third—the Caslakes must be literally sailing past their front door at this point—then *Kathi Anne*, upright in the still air and looking uncomfortably held in, her old dowager self today. She tacks across *Amasonia*'s stern, a slow, skating turn, then, past the ferry dock, picks up and leans as David finds a patch of wind somewhere out there on the grey mirror.

With the other cars I drive through La Have and take the rutted dirt track out to Fort Point—Fort Sainte Marie de Grace, the Lunenburg County Historical Society tells us, built in 1632. There is a grey shingled cottage with historical display cases and a volunteer pleased to have visitors. There is a parking lot, a flagpole, a navigation light facing the bay and a mid-nineteenth-century cannon, but the fort has long since settled into the earth.

In the water directly below us a brown head appears and begins swimming along parallel to the shore, trailing its long hair in the water. When I point the swimmer out to Mort Pelham, he identifies it as a grey seal and launches into a testy lecture on their destructiveness—they eat fish, shellfish, damage fishing gear. The punchline is, they are protected by the government. Best not to be a federal man in these parts.

Mort Pelham goes back to his car. With several visitors— from their accents tourists from the States—I watch a chorus line of four boats—*Margaret Anne*, *Kathi Anne*, *Amasonia* and *Sebim*—bunched on the same port tack, approach us from the lee shore. *Margaret Anne* is the farthest upwind and is pulling ahead of her sister ship, causing one of the visitors to remark, "I can tell right now which skipper is the best." I ask him which, and he indicates the natural wood boat. I tell him to keep an eye on the turquoise. When I explain that they are father and son, and that the father, who is seventy-seven, singlehandedly built both boats, he looks at me in disbelief. By the time we look back to the water David has tacked twice, in some mysterious way edging past the *Margaret Anne*, and is heading out for Bull Rock.

The yacht club at one-thirty in the afternoon has the air of a small railway station between trains—nothing is going to happen until three-thirty, perhaps not then. Several retired couples—the Pelhams are one—eat lunch or talk quietly in the lounge corner. The club operator-bartender sits on the back porch, outside the screen door, smoking. The near corner of the room reverberates with the red and yellow sounds of Space Invaders, as two eight-year-olds pursue its endless string of explosions, harmless as water drops but noisier in the high-ceilinged room. If these electronic drops were the buzzing of flies it could be a summer afternoon in 1884.

After lunch I drive back down the river looking for sails — it is three o'clock, the time at which, on previous afternoons, we were crossing the finish line — but the river is empty. At Fort Point I scan the rim of La Have Bay. There are two sails, so distant they are like periods of white ink on grey paper. I walk down along the shore, spending a pleasant hour among the seagrass and boulders, picking up smooth blue stones that have the shapes of fish or hulls. They sit on my desk now, holding down papers and reminding me of the broken shore of La Have Bay and of all the town-dump detritus the sea throws up in stone, glass, wood, styrofoam and empty, partial sea-shells.

After an hour, the one dot has come within recognition range and proves to be a fiberglass sloop that has given up its daysail in this stationary weather and is motoring in. The other, which by its mound profile — at a great distance, the three sails fuse into a small hill of white — I am pretty sure is a schooner, has gotten smaller and I decide it is not the first boat coming in, but the last going out. This race will be longer than anyone thought.

After a trip to Bridgewater I return to the club around six to find that the Old Gaffers Race, the shorter of the two being sailed today, has been called off for lack of wind. The Premier's Cup would be called too but the *Kathi Anne* and one or two other boats have no radios.

The *Margaret Anne* was the lead boat in the Old Gaffers, and Murray Stevens stands in the midst of a crowd in the club room, his kit bags at his feet, entertaining them with his problems. "We were heading for Pollock Shoal and trying to get through the channel there between West Ironbound and the mainland — and we would tack and then tack back — and we'd be in the same place! And we'd do it again and we were *still* in the same place. Couldn't make headway. Well finally we said what's the point of this?"

Murray Stevens is forty-seven years old, a chunky, blond, smiling man who laughs more than his father and is clearly energized by being in a crowd. He is heavier-set than David and has a large head with prominent features, emphasized by the fact that his curly blond hair covers only the back half of his head, giving him a great arch of forehead over his long face. In one respect he resembles his father exactly: he has the same large hands with broad blunt fingers that you feel would close on a two-by-four as if it were a broom handle. In the years that he has carried on the boatbuilding business, Murray has become as renowned as his father and is himself the subject of magazine articles that dub him "Canada's finest boatbuilder." Murray's largest boat, the seventy-seven-foot schooner *Raindancer*, was built in 1980, largely of a dark, hard, tropical wood called angelique. "She took up the whole middle of Murray's shop," David Callan recalls, "and the angelique was so hard they had to sharpen the saw blades after every third cut." Recently put up for sale by her owner, the advertisement in *Wooden Boat* magazine described *Raindancer* as "from the famous yard of Murray Stevens in Lunenburg, Nova Scotia."

Ralph Tingley and his crew are preparing a lobster cook-out on the front lawn of the club. The large pot of water has begun heating over a portable gas flame, and two youngsters at the picnic table play a bit hard-heartedly with the groggy lobsters as if they were stuffed bears or airplanes.

I reintroduce myself to Murray and ask for some time to sit and talk with him. "Excuse me for tonight," he says. "Six hours of concentration skippering a boat wipes me out. I'm exhausted." We arrange to meet after the races tomorrow. I have dinner from the club kitchen and eat at a table facing Miller Head, partly to keep an eye out for sails, partly to ignore the fate of the by now much-used lobsters. When darkness comes, around eight o'clock, most of the boats from both races have given up and motored in. *Kathi Anne* and *Sorceress*, the report is, are still sailing and are not yet even in the river.

*Saturday.*   The last day of Schooner Race Week couldn't be less auspicious. It is raining in that steady, determined way that seems to promise forty days and forty nights. In addition, the river is filled with fog that moves mysteriously back and forth over water that is a green mud color and smooth as a seal's back or belly. The forecast on the radio this morning was for winds fifteen to twenty-five knots in the morning, tailing off in the afternoon, but there is no sign of it in the slowly revolving green riverscape outside the windows.

People are making a late start of it this morning. It is nine-fifteen and only a few small groups are scattered around at the tables eating breakfast. Yesterday's race ended, I learn, at one in the morning, when the wind finally sprang up and *Kathi Anne* and *Sorceress* crossed the line within minutes of each other. All told, the final two competitors raced for fourteen hours, a record for the Schooner Association and for David Stevens, who has not appeared yet this morning, although he usually comes across on the eight-thirty ferry at La Have. If he were another seventy-seven-year-old, I would expect him to spend the day in bed.

I have a cup of coffee and pass some time reading the bulletin board. One section is notices from people offering to crew or simply wanting to go along on the races — every approach from the direct "I would like to crew — [name]," to the neatly hand-lettered card, "Fun-loving southern lady, on vacation from South Carolina, very limited sailing experience, offers herself as first-class above-deck ballast during Schooner Race Week." There is a flyer for "Women's Sailing '84," Laser races in Dartmouth and Quebec City, and I note that "BYOB" in this country means bring your own boat. Next to it is a routine but more sober message, "Overdue Notice. Sailing Vessel —

*Shanghi Lil*, white with gold mast, last sighted in vicinity of Sable Island or Cape Sable Island on July l4th. Owner—A. Mosher (New Jersey). Any info Phone RCC Halifax, 426-4730 collect." I hope for *Shanghi Lil* that it was Cape Sable Island down the coast toward Yarmouth. Sable Island is quite a different matter. A barren spit of sand 170 miles out in the Atlantic, it is, because of a peculiar combination of tides and reefs, one of the graveyards of the Atlantic, its waters the resting place of more than two hundred ships collected over the last three centuries. A map of Sable Island showing all the wrecks looks like a long, thin microrganism with cilia.

My attention is caught by a collection of old silver on a shelf over the Franklin stove in the lounge corner. Today is trophy day—the presentation of the week's awards will be after the race this afternoon—so the trophies have been returned by last year's winners and make a bright pile of bowls, trays, mugs and loving cups on the shelf, rather like a Victorian wedding table. The silver is old-fashioned in style, the Oland Tray heavily embossed with the familiar patterns of grape foliage, the Old Gaffers Trophy fittingly a bowl with a scalloped and heavily encrusted lip. One, the largest loving cup, seems genuinely old. The silver plate is wearing thin and the engraving around the base is dim and hard to read: "Colonial Fisheries, Ltd. Awarded to Capt. Angus Walters—outstanding fishing Schooner Bluenose—Winner of International Fisherman's Race—Halifax, N.S. Oct. 22, 24, 25, 1921." It is the trophy from *Bluenose's* first race. When the schooner races were revived in the 1970s, it was put up by Captain Walters as a boat-for-boat trophy. It will go to the first boat across the line in today's race.

I join several of the Stevens grandchildren who are having a sleepy breakfast over by the front windows and ask them about the long race yesterday. They tell me *Sebim* was the first of the Premier's Cup boats to motor in, around dark. David did not consider it because he was unsure if his motor was working—on the trip from Second Peninsula last weekend it had sputtered once and died. He thought that if he even tried to start it he would be forfeiting the race. This is not true, the kids say — you are not out until you start motoring — but the truth seems to be that David preferred to keep sailing.

In fourteen hours they had consumed everything there was to eat on board, down to and including the last package of dried soup. With nothing else to do, hour after hour in the drifting match, someone put out a line and caught two pollock, but David threw them back. They are a red-meat fish and he doesn't care for them. After fourteen hours adrift, an hour or more within spitting distance of the finish line, they got wind and ended by tying up in a gale, caught by surprise at the buoy with all their sails up.

About a quarter to ten David arrives, looking lively and alert, although he pantomimes his head as "out to here."

"Now you know what a hangover is like," Bart says.

"I had to make two dives for the door this morning to get my head through."

"What are you doing here?" Mort Pelham says to David.

"Just got in a little while ago," David replies and, looking through the front windows at the solidifying wall of green fog, "I don't think we'll race today. Too dangerous at the start in this. We've won enough this week, anyway."

Half an hour later I get David into an old, collapsed chair in the lounge area and settle into one next to him. On the last day of Schooner Race Week I want to get his comments on the various races, but when I ask him about the Monday race, he says, "That was the Oland Tray. We had a fair good breeze — and — we won it. You were there." — and then, seeing that I am expecting more — "That's about all I remember. Some skippers re-race it and re-race it in the club, and so on. I just forget about it. Just another race." He does answer my questions, however, and his detailed replies about the battle for Bull Rock mark on Monday and the perils of the fog around False La Have on Tuesday indicate that no lessons are lost from the races he sails. But the one race that seems to crowd out everything else in his mind is yesterday's long-distance drifter, and he keeps coming back to it throughout the conversation as if it were the only race of the week, as if he were still moved by something about those long hours on the water.

"Last night we made dozens and dozens of tacks and, yeah, half a dozen or more jibes, just picking every little bit of wind I could detect on the side of my face. It was dark so you couldn't see anything in the water, no ripples that you get even from the slightest breeze, and my dad also he would sit facing forward and he'd go by the wind on the side of his face. And that's what I was doing last night, and it's amazing, I still have to *wonder* how I got her in this distance with no wind at all and a falling tide."

"Tide and current going the other way."

"Going out against me. There was one time, over at Riverport, there was a red light on the end of the dock there and it almost seemed to be slipping backwards, and I wondered if I'd be able to make it. She's an amazing boat." He pauses for a moment, looking out the windows at the fog, and, although he does not actually smile, the lines around his eyes lengthen. "I can almost talk to her and she'll do what I want her to."

"You must have been pretty tired last night," I venture. "People were coming in here who had been out six and eight hours and they were wiped out."

"Well, they're only young fellows," he says with obvious satisfaction.

"So, how did you do it for fourteen?"

"I guess I'm conceited. It's a race and I'm responsible for everything—the safety—and it's my duty to be at the wheel, and look out. And I've had years of taking that responsibility and it doesn't come hard. And it reminded me," he pauses, then goes on with pleasure, "I told the crew last night, this night sailing like this reminded me so much of when I sailed in the Great Lakes. Many's the night I spent all night on deck alone. Oh yes, sailing across the lake a hundred, hundred-and-fifty-mile trips. The rest of the party would be down below sleeping and I'd be there alone on deck. Till after daylight. Oh yes. But last night was fun, because I had company, people to talk to."

I can't believe how chipper he is. He turns and greets Francine, who approaches a chair across from us rather gingerly. "Poor gal, you've taken a lot of punishment to get through this week."

"Oh, I'm all right."

"Are you?"

"Yes," her habitual laugh helps to revive her. "This is Saturday. I'll hold up."

Andy King, a retired sailor who, like Mort Pelham, comes around to enjoy the camaraderie before and after the races, comes up to us. "You fellows just going to do some hard looking today?"

I expect David to agree but he says instead, "I wouldn't say that."

"No?"

"I passed the *Kathi Anne* over to a new skipper." We look surprised, except for Francine, who looks pleased and nervous. "Bart Shea is taking her out."

"Oh," says Andy King, and I get the feeling this is something of a bombshell. Later David confirms that he has never allowed anyone else to skipper the *Kathi Anne* in a race.

Francine glances toward the windows where the fog seems a bit more translucent, "Are we going if it's foggy?"

"Talk to Bart," David replies, playing his new underling status.

"You are going to navigate for him?"

"Well, I'll tell him where the river is," he says, drawing a laugh from Francine's worry. "Sure I'll navigate."

A few minutes later, David is standing with a group of sailors, telling the end of yesterday's race: "Well, *Sorceress* beat us on corrected time. We were almost at the line and she was back down at Fort Point, when she picked up the wind there. She brought it all the way up the river with her, and by the time it hit us, she was practically here."

The men laugh and I notice a newcomer among them. He is as short as David, and his small frame and sloping shoulders, together with his wide smile, give him a friendly, unaggressive look, so I am surprised when he is introduced to me as Warren Doane. This is the infamous master of *Sebim*, the man who commissioned her specifically to beat the *Kathi Anne*, the black hat who has engaged the Stevens clan in a ten-year tussle for dominance of the schooner races. Warren Doane, the arch-rival, standing by the kitchen counter sharing jokes with David, seems about as fierce as the neighborhood postman, but I learn a bit later he is sailing on *Sebim* today, at the invitation of the new owner, and wonder if this has anything to do with getting David out on the water.

At the skippers' meeting, Ralph Tingley has more explaining than usual to do. In addition to the two trophies up today—the Colonial Fisheries, the boat-for-boat trophy, and the *Herald and Mail* for the first on corrected time—they are rerunning the Old Gaffers, cancelled yesterday.

"Only the Old Gaffers who were registered yesterday can participate," Ralph calls.

The race will be entirely in the river today, in deference to the light and uncertain winds. After yesterday's race someone had questioned, not too gently, the wisdom of scheduling the longest race of the week on the day with the least wind. Today no one will be becalmed way out, and the length of the race will be controlled.

"You go down the river to the Riverport marks," Ralph explains, "green and red to starboard, the stakes. There's a green stake first and then a red, go around them to starboard—yes—and then you come up river and if we're real late, we'll stop. If you hear a gun, stop."

"What do you mean, stop?"

"If the leader gets a gun, that's the end of the race. If you don't hear a gun keep going upriver. There's a mark about a mile up on this side, at Trevorsee—quite close to the shore—and then there's one on the other shore a little farther down. Just starboard, starboard and then do the line again, and if we've still got a bit of wind, we'll repeat. If you don't hear the gun, go around again."

There is a buzz in the room as the adjustable course is

explained and re-explained from table to table. Finally everyone seems satisfied and Ralph welcomes a new skipper and boat to the races, Richard Harrison with *Windhawk*.

"For those of you who are interested, there were just two times in yesterday's race. *Kathi Anne* at twelve, fifty-four, fifty, and *Sorceress* at one, one, twenty." Someone says, "They both had the same breeze," which draws a laugh, David's story having made the rounds, and the meeting breaks up.

We cast off and make our way quietly upriver. The greenish fog has lifted to the level of the treetops, like a curtain rising part way in a theatre, revealing patches of rough surface on the water that grow and begin to join in a breeze not much stronger than a breath. There is no feeling of hurrying this morning. The lively gavotte in which the schooners circle one another upstream of the line, one-eyeing each other for advantage, keeping the other on the starting line, has become a minuet in slow motion, the sails limp and stately, their masts brushing the underside of the fog as if it were a ceiling. We all seem still a bit sleepy under that blanket. Conversation flows back and forth between the boats in easy periods as they glide past, the water, as it will on a glassy day, amplifying the voices. We elicit a stream of banter moving through the fleet as the other crews spot Bart at the wheel and David standing, feet spread, hands on hips, on the afterdeck between the backstays.

"Who's the new flunk?" someone says for the fourth time, and David answers again, "Well, I've been demoted."

"Helm alee," Bart calls and swings us over to a port tack, heading back downriver into the wind. "Awfully light today. Better stay close to the line." Bart appears easy; if he has any butterflies at the prospect of racing David's boat with David aboard, he does not reveal them. *Sebim* passes us, moving confidently upstream with Warren Doane at the wheel, confirming our assumption — that he has been invited to skipper the final race, to redeem *Sebim*'s performance.

The ten-minute gun sounds and Bart checks the time with David Peill, who has taken over the time-keeping job. We are light on crew today. Murray's kids are sailing the *Margaret*

*Anne*, as they did yesterday, and we are also missing Peter and Mike Peill. When David said he wasn't racing today, they chose to sleep in and are bedded down over on Second Peninsula, oblivious to the change in plan. We have the remaining Peills, Rob, Eddie and David, and Francine, who gets to crew today to make up six. I am the sole passenger.

As the starting gun goes off, *Kathi Anne*'s bow is right on the line with half a dozen others equally spread to port and starboard. We are dead center in the pack, the wind, such as it is, coming from downriver, off the starboard bow, and in a moment we are wind-surrounded, with sails on all sides, and *Margaret Anne* directly upwind, shadowing us. We drift forward as a group.

Fifteen minutes later the fog has cleared and we are spread out evenly over the river, halfway to La Have, a flotilla of patient, upright white sails. David says, "Look at *Sebim*," and we look over to the eastern shore in time to see her turning abruptly to port. A moment later *Amasonia* makes the same move, and thirty seconds after that we understand why as our sails begin their dry rattling and the wind moves around to head us.

Leaving La Have to starboard we are pointed toward Riverport, diagonally across the river and at the base of an indentation called Ritcey Cove. We have passed *Sebim*, *Adare* and *Margaret Anne*, who have had to tack to stay off the eastern shore. Only *Amasonia*, the slim little marconi, can point high enough into the wind that she continues to slip up along the boulder line of the eastern shore, ahead of us by four boat lengths as we steer the center of the channel. Looking in the direction of the gut, off our starboard bow, I see a white wall of fog sitting on the water; a fresh, cold wind comes out of it, like a wind off a glacier. The fog proceeds across the center of Ritcey Cove and meets the shore just beyond where *Amasonia* is sailing, the white bar bending up slightly as it climbs the shore and crosses the road and the line of Victorian houses facing the water. The houses on this side of the bar are sharp and solid, on the other side fading into a grainy winter distance. *Amasonia* begins pointing up and we too, as the cold wind hits, sheet in and point up toward the fog.

The wind continues to build and *Kathi Anne*, on her favorite windward tack, takes off with an acceleration that, even after a week of racing on this boat, surprises me. Passing another boat is normally a patient business, drawn out over a period of minutes, of creeping up, edging past. This time the wind hits us first and we pass *Amasonia* as if she were pulled off looking for a place to park and leave her by a good six boat lengths, and the rest of the fleet by a quarter-mile, as the fog, a cold hand over the face, coats the world around us.

We can still see about fifty yards ahead, and a moment after we enter the fog our lookout spots the red and green stakes directly ahead. Bart runs past the green stake by four boat lengths, then calls "Helm alee!" and we come about in as sharp a blow as we've had all week and head across the channel, whipping around the red stake and back up river, the wind behind us pushing us out of the fog into the clear world again. *Amasonia* and *Margaret Anne*, our immediate competitors, cut close around the green stake and head immediately for the red, where they come about to follow us. It is not as effective a maneuver; they lose some headway at the red stake, and by the time they are heading back up river after us, they are a hundred yards back.

We are now presented with a formal review of sail. The boats have fallen into a line, working up on a tight starboard tack to the green and red stakes: *Amasonia* and *Margaret Anne* behind us, already bent around the marks; then *Hebridee*, *Sebim*, *Adare*, *Windhawk*, *Hakada*, *Sorceress*, the *Maid of Uist*, *Elsie L*, in single file, all closed up, bright beads on a string. As we sail back down the line, the reviewing boat, we can look over and watch each one sail from the clear water of the cove up into the veil of fog, going suddenly dusty as an old photograph, around the stakes, leaning in the violent wind that is storming there, then emerging back into the brighter air, joining the line going back upriver. It is like one of those artist's conceptions, showing day and night and day again as the earth revolves. And for all the damp chill of the fog, the grey water, the lowering sky, it is still a stirring sight — eleven schooners in a line. It recalls other times when these boats were the symbol of connection with foreign lands, of adventure, of heading out, were part of the sinew that knit empire. Brittania ruled the waves. Watching the line of sail it isn't hard to imagine martial music, or a thump of guns as they would salute one another across the water, arriving with goods and stories from ports as far as Aukland and Melbourne, an exact hemisphere away.

Thirty minutes later, we are halfway back to the yacht club in the long forearm of the La Have River and the wind has disappeared again. Glassy. The boats are spread across the river, sails wung out at their most expansive to catch whatever last tags and tails of wind there are. *Amasonia* and *Margaret Anne* are across on the eastern shore and even with us. You can call where we are dead center — dead, anyway.

David says, "It's going to come off the land any minute now," but this time his forecasting powers have deserted him. The surface remains smooth. The fleet is coming up on us, *Adare*, *Sebim*, *Hebridee*, *Hakada* spread across the river. If *Kathi Anne* took off like a kestrel into the heading wind at the mouth of the river, running before this light trailing wind is her poorest, heaviest quarter. She seems almost to dig in her heels.

*Margaret Anne* and *Amasonia* have a bit of wind on the eastern shore and have pulled ahead. Bored, Francine and David engage in an extended banter, each trying to out-flunky the other. Bart seems cool at the helm, watching his sails for the slightest twitch. Glassy.

*Sebim* has come up on our port stern, as if she could not run this race without seeking out her old rival at some point, and the two large boats crawl up the river, working closer and closer to the western shore. *Sebim* tries to pass us but the best she can do is pull even.

"I think I'll drive him up a little," Bart says, "see how good a helmsman he is." He swings *Kathi Anne* a bit to port, and the two boats work farther in to shore. We are alone here—the rest of the fleet, led by *Margaret Anne*, *Amasonia* and now *Hebridee*, are in the center of the river.

We are in the shadow of Miller Head. The sun has appeared from behind broken clouds and, coming through the trees, penetrates the still water to several feet below the surface, giving it a dense green look. Through this jungle-like stillness the two large boats move on what seems to be a memory of breeze. So silent is it, so delicate the progress of the two boats moving at the exact same speed, that conversations on board are in an undertone, or whispered. I can look across a few yards of water and see the slight, white-haired figure of Warren Doane, standing at the helm of *Sebim*, all his attention forward. There is no talk between boats, although a word would carry, just the concentration of all eyes and minds on the two hulls slipping through the water, the stillness, the focus of an operating room.

The clubhouse has come into sight. *Sebim*, summoning wind from somewhere, has cleared Miller Head and is up by eight boat lengths and heading for the line. We wait for the sound—if there is a gun at this point it is all over—but there is only silence from the shore, and *Sebim* continues upriver, followed by *Margaret Anne*, now crossing the line, her varnished wood hull glowing in the new sunlight, and *Amasonia* close behind her. We are suddenly fourth in the procession we have been leading for an hour.

When the breeze comes, it comes upriver and takes us with it—a repeat of the Friday night finish. As we approach *Amasonia*'s stern, we shadow her from the wind, not letting her have it until we have slipped by her port side, leaving her a present of it too late to be of use. We take the *Margaret Anne* in the same way, slipping around to port as, up ahead, *Sebim* jibes around the first stake and heads across the river for the second.

Our jibe is a scramble with a crew of only six—I am given a line to hold for a moment until someone with two other jobs can tie it off—but it is accomplished and we head for the eastern shore on a reach in a light but increasingly steady wind.

The river has begun to narrow at this point on its way to Bridgewater, is only about a quarter of a mile wide, and the line of four big boats — *Sebim*, *Kathi Anne*, *Margaret Anne* and *Amasonia* — fills it with sail from bank to bank. As we go across we look back at a right angle to the string of boats still coming upriver to the first mark.

We are close on *Sebim*'s stern as she approaches the stake near the eastern shore, and when she wings a bit wide going around, Bart pulls the *Kathi Anne* inside her as smoothly as a city driver changing lanes. We are to windward of her and pointing up comfortably for the center of the line — it is only a matter of seconds before we are past her and in clear water.

"Shows you what this boat can do when you give her a chance," David mutters quietly, as *Sebim* swings across our stern to get to windward and *Margaret Anne* follows suit.

Bart answers blandly, "Just want to sail my own race."

As we approach the finish line the wind shifts, as happens so frequently in this frustrating river, and we have to fall off to port. It will take another tack to reach the line.

David makes a staying gesture with his hand, but Bart says, "Have to go now. *Sebim* is coming," and we come about to a port tack, sailing across *Sebim*'s bow by fifty yards at the center of the line.

Again, a gun here would end the race, and for a moment we hold our breaths, anticipating the report, but the line is crossed silently and we swing back upriver for one more go around.

We jibe around the western stake. *Sebim*, close on our stern, tries to pass to windward on the reach across the channel. There is a nerved quiet about being the leader and pursued. The crew move lightly about the deck, performing economically but in total silence. They almost never look behind. The hiss of *Sebim*'s bow wave is the only sound accompanying their work.

We come about onto a port tack at the eastern mark, and as the crew trims in carefully, Bart says, "Let's go for home."

*Sebim* does not tack and follow us back across toward the yacht club. Instead, Warren Doane swings her down parallel to the eastern shore and the two boats begin to diverge. There is a racing strategy that says essentially, if you can't beat 'em, don't join 'em — that is, if you can't beat a boat on its own tack, strike out on another — you might get lucky. *Sebim* moves away along the boulder-lined shore.

*Kathi Anne* has been crossing the center of the river directly toward the line of tailenders moving up to the western stake, and now we come about to stay out of their windshadow. At the same time *Sebim*, on the eastern shore, comes about to a port tack and we head toward each other on the criss-cross pattern that we followed in Wednesday's tacking duel. At the first meeting we cross her by about fifty yards, but as we come about to port and she counters with a starboard tack, David squints into the sun and says, "She gained a little on us."

Gone is the flunky humor, gone his vacationing air trimming sail and loosening the backstays. He is concentrating again on wind, water, current, tide, and all his clocks are running. It is not lack of confidence in Bart, just the instinct, once trained, never still.

David tells a story on himself of a race several years ago in Mahone Bay: "It was Saturday, the last race, and we'd won quite a few times that week, so I figured, today we'll hang back, just sail along behind the pack, enjoy ourselves. We had a lot of passengers on board. Evelyn was there, Florence, Murray's wife. Well, when the gun went off I looked at Murray — and he looked at me — and I said, 'All passengers below!' and 'Everyone to stations!' I just couldn't *not* respond to that gun."

"And did you win?"

He thinks back, then looks a bit surprised, "I believe we did."

We cross *Sebim* again at about the same distance but our nerves make it seem less. To add to the feeling of pack pursuit, *Margaret Anne* is on a parallel tack to us and seems to be closing and *Amasonia* is heading down the river directly for us. David Peill, perhaps the most worldly and relaxed of all the Peill sons, sits on top of the cabin, regarding the busy water behind us full of sails and says over and over under his breath,

"*Come on, come on, come on,* Kathi Anne." Barely audible, it is the only cheering I have heard all week.

But this is the last race and we are ahead and we want to win. David looks at the yacht club coming up ahead, then looks calculatingly back at the outside marker of the finish line and finally cannot contain himself. It is David who says, "Ready about!" and Bart responds with "Helm alee!" spinning the wheel and bringing us over to a starboard tack. We point toward the outside mark but will not quite make it on this tack. *Sebim* is parallel now but four boat lengths downwind. Just beyond the outside buoy, we come about to port within twenty yards of the line and the wind expires. As we have so many times that week, we and the *Kathi Anne* sit upright in the water and wait, and do a little praying. The wind returns — it could not have been more than thirty seconds — but from the direction of the club, taking us along parallel to the line.

David looks upstream at the full collection of sail and says, "Every second counts." He is thinking of *Amasonia* and corrected time.

"Helm alee," Bart calls. We have gained enough headway to come about to starboard and cross the last twenty yards to the invisible line. When the gun sounds from shore there is a general exhaling of tension, grins along the deck. It is the closest finish we have had. David turns to the skipper with a wicked smile and says what has been delicately unspoken all week. "All you have to do is stop smoking, Bart."

Bart grins back his double-row, Teddy Roosevelt grin, "That little bit of a push on that last mark, that was my reward."

It is an hour later and we are all ashore. The trophies have been moved out onto a picnic table on the front lawn of the club. They make a brilliant silver mound reflecting the afternoon sky and water. A strong, late wind has sprung up, washing the sky clean and dramatically roughing the surface of the water so that it is, looking eastward with the sun at our backs, blue-black, four shades darker than the sky. The silver bowls and cups stand out against it, as do the double masts of the schooners tied up a dozen feet below the lawn at the floating docks.

I sit on the concrete lip of the front porch with Kent Nason, who has brought all his camera equipment along to record the award ceremonies, and we stare out at the incomparably vivid light as it begins to yellow into late afternoon, progressively gilding a scene that is already largely memory, La Have '84, the Schooner Races.

The officials at the ceremony, Dave Waterbury and Ed Murphy, wear uniforms, navy blue blazers and skippers' caps, white shirts and navy blue ties with a discreet pattern of white sails, on the jacket pockets the insignia of the Schooner Association. A sizeable crowd sits on the porch, on lawn chairs and picnic tables to both sides, with kids and limber people sprawling on the grass in front. Bottles of beer pass freely among the drinkers, jokes and cheerful talk among everyone. Dave Waterbury, speaking into a bull horn, gives a brief welcome and introduction, then gets right to the first trophy, which is the Oland Tray to *Kathi Anne* for Monday's race. David Stevens comes out of the crowd, bareheaded and dressed in a bulky, navy blue skipper's jacket. He looks rather like a child who has been bundled up by his mother, but that, I decide, is less the over-sized jacket than the subdued, embarrassed manner in which he takes the tray, shakes Ed Murphy's hand with a polite word of thanks, as if he did not know him, and fades back into the crowd.

The others get more pleasure out of their awards, Ed Murphy collecting the Cooley Mugs from his co-host; the eight members of the crew of *Sorceress* coming up en masse for the Pullen Trophy, then for the Premier's Cup, in yellow teeshirts that say "*Sorceress*" and have her picture on them; Ralph Tingley waving the fun trophy, a bottle of liquor in a plastic shopping bag, as three young women with cameras run up and kneel on the lawn, as if on cue, to take his picture. Murray comes up to accept the Old Gaffers Trophy, which he has won frequently in the past. He gets a laugh with a reference to

Friday's aborted race. "It took me a long time to win it this year."

Interspersed with these awards and the familiar jibes and jokes from the crowd, David trudges up to collect, in addition to the Oland Tray, the Memorial Trophy (Tuesday in the fog), the McGaskill picture (Wednesday), the *Herald and Mail* Trophy (today, corrected time) and finally the Colonial Fisheries Trophy from the *Bluenose*'s first race (today, boat-for-boat). He is embarrassed at having so much hardware and seems cut off from the easy camaraderie of the other winners—even Sonny Nauss, coming up to accept a sole second prize for *Sebim* in the *Herald and Mail* race, draws a good-natured laugh with "At least we got something out of it." It is a camaraderie that David shares easily, standing around in the clubhouse before a race. Now he has no words; he seems isolated with all his silver, and after several awards takes his crew up with him and passes the cups and trays into other hands.

As the ceremonies break up, Kent Nason lines up David and his crew for a formal photograph. All the crew members except Bart are wearing *Kathi Anne* polo shirts now, navy blue with white collars and white emblems with pictures of the boat on them. One row stands; the other kneels; and holding the collection of ornate silver, the young men, with their full mustaches, so serious, so upright, look like a varsity team from a century ago.

The crowd has mostly dispersed, and I have finally gotten together with Murray as we arranged yesterday. We are about to sit down at one of the picnic tables on the front lawn of the club when David comes over to say goodbye. He is driving home to Second Peninsula, will come back tomorrow with all the Peill grandsons to sail the *Kathi Anne* around and into her home mooring. We chat for a moment about my trip back—I am planning to stop at Lyndhurst, the Peill farm in the Annapolis Valley, to be shown their "intensive management" wheat crops, before making the evening ferry for Bar Harbor, Maine. I thank him for allowing me to sail with him and then, overstating a bit in my enthusiasm, say, "David, do you realize you won every race this week?"

"Well now, we didn't win every race," he says with his persistent accuracy, "but we were first across the line in every race." Then, after a moment's thought, "I believe that's a record."

David waves and walks off toward his ten-year-old Dodge in the dirt parking lot beside the club. Murray and I slide into the plank seats on opposite sides of the picnic table. He has sat facing into the sun, which is just above the treetops behind the yacht club's roof, and after a couple of questions and answers I ask him if he would be more comfortable sitting the other way.

"No, that's all right," he says. "I'll just squint a bit." Staring into the horizontal bars of the sun, his eyes narrowed as if he were sighting a long distance across water, he talks about growing up on Second Peninsula, about laying keels in the boatshop, and about his father, David, and his grandfather, Randolph.

# THE
# GENERATIONS

"*I* call him 'a gentleman of the heart.' And if you had known my grandfather, you'd understand why he produced a son like Daddy, because he was a super, super man." It is Dorothy Peill talking. "And he wasn't, you know, educated to be a gentleman as you think of them—private schools and all this—he simply was born a gentleman."

"This is your father?"

"My grandfather. This is Randolph Stevens."

Murray too, although I start out at the picnic table in front of the yacht club asking about his father, slides easily, as if the question required it, into talking about his grandfather. "He was an extremely gentle person, one that—his word was respected at all times. He only spoke once, in a low voice, and he was both understood and obeyed."

I think of David giving commands in that flat, indoor voice, from the helm of the *Kathi Anne*.

"When he moved across the deck, you never even felt the

boat jiggle. I always tell my crew, when you're pulling in a sail in a light air you must pull it in *very gently*. And when you're walking across a deck, you should walk across it as a butterfly." Murray smiles at the image of his grandfather crossing the deck. His eyes crinkle into the sun. "I spent a lot of time with him. I used to go down to the sail loft in the evenings — while he was sewing sails. He used to hand-rope all of the sails at that time. And I used to go down and lay back on a sail bag and there'd be people coming and going — and they'd be telling stories and talking about the old days and all of a sudden that would remind him of a certain verse in Scott or Burns, and he would quote for ten or fifteen minutes perhaps."

"Poetry?"

"He had only a grade two education. He spent several years in grade two but never graduated because he always had to go fishing in the spring before the exams. And when he was nine years old, of course, he had to go to the Banks. But he was blessed with one thing, and that was a photographic memory. While he was doing sails, he always had a book of Scott or a book of poems by his side, and he would read a verse and then he would sew a while, and over the years he had memorized — oh, I suppose — twenty or thirty hours of different poems. He could go on hour after hour."

David, speaking slowly, his emphatic voice: "Every meal since I can remember, every evening meal, he had the Bible and he read a chapter. And in my bringing up, I think he read it over a couple of times. And you can imagine, with ten or twelve children around the table, after he finished a chapter we'd all start to jammer back and forth, and he'd take his knife," David lifts one of his broad-bladed fingers, "and tap it twice on the table," *thump, thump*, "and you could hear a pin drop. Then he'd say grace."

"There were few like him." This is Harold talking. "Most fearless man in boats and around the water I ever knew. Never changing, even-tempered. I guess you could call him conservative — he had a strong feeling toward empire, toward the goodness of life in Canada due to the British Empire. He was a man of fair dealing," Harold says mildly but with conviction, "a great man."

"We always said it was because Harold was born in a sail loft, his father's sail loft on Tancook." Mary Dauphinee is talking. "It's true. Father was repairing the house and Mother was pregnant with Harold, so when it got near time, the loft was clean and spacious and full of light; they moved there. And the sights and smells of that loft stayed right with him, were imprinted on his mind from birth. Harold always wanted to be a sailmaker."

He has heard the story many times and just smiles, "Oh, I don't know, I just liked working at it. When I was twelve, Father used to get me to stand behind the machine and pull the cloth. It was an old Singer and not powerful enough to pull all that weight. I must have pulled it pretty good because he selected me again. It was a year or two later he built the loft here—half the present building. Sailmaking was different in those days. We used Egyptian cotton—long staple cotton, a fine, fine cloth. No shaping; you just cut it out and sew it together and rope it. In the 1950s we began shaping sails because Dacron came along and that wouldn't stretch. Egyptian cotton and canvas stretched, and that made the shape."

"I had worked around the boatshop always," Murray is saying, "up bothering my father and all the workmen, trying to get at the vise, always, to make small boats. After school I never used to spend much time in the house. I tried to get right into the boatshop and see what the men had done during the day."

Like his father and grandfather, although for somewhat different reasons, Murray Stevens has worked at a series of jobs, or "phases" of his life, as he terms them. After graduating from Lunenburg Academy, the local high school, he apprenticed for a year in a steel fabrication plant in Germany owned by Jock Peill's family, then returned to Nova Scotia and enrolled in Acadia University. "There's many things that I'm very interested in, but English composition, at that particular time, was not one of them. After one year," he says with a chuckle that seems genuinely amused, "I wasn't invited back for a second."

He went back to work in the boatshop for a year or two, then in 1960 married Florence and went into the real-estate-assessment business, earning a degree from Dalhousie University. During his years as a tax assessor he located Lyndhurst, the rolling, rich farm in the tidal basin at the head of the Annapolis Valley, where Jock and Dorothy Peill have settled and made their complex of farm businesses. In 1965 the government moved to take over tax assessment, requiring all existing assessors to become civil servants. At the same time, David Stevens moved to get his son back into the boat business, helping him to build his modern, glass-walled house on the crest of the hill of David's land. Together they went to Expo in 1967 and built the *Atlantica*.

"The problems of building on site were really quite staggering. I used to go down to the hardware store in the city two or three mornings a week and carry armloads of sandpaper and paint and supplies over through the Metro. And it was a terrible jostle, with a big box of stuff, because, of course, everyone was going over there to the fair and it was a jam-packed Metro. Well, we survived—and that was another phase—another phase of the whole job."

Wooden boats are a luxury, built plank by plank in an age when they can be molded from fiberglass in a fraction of the time, producing identical clones of hulls that wooden boat people refer to, with a note of feisty contempt, as "Tupperware." Wood still has many advantages over fiberglass, not the least the pure aesthetic pleasure of its silence as it slips through the water, but in a decade of stagnation for the Canadian economy the wooden boat business has come to a standstill. After the great angelique schooner *Raindancer* in 1980, Murray's shop, like his father's before him, has survived by picking up whatever variety of business was there—an extensive rebuilding job on *Bluenose II*; a pair of signal poles, tall as masts on a square-rigger, for the Citadel, the historic fortress in Halifax; maintenance, winter storage, welding.

"My next project, small project, is to do a piece of—I guess you'd call it art work—in stainless steel. It's a weathervane for the top of the new World Trade Center in Halifax—a stylized *Bluenose*, sitting on top of a five-foot stainless-steel globe. I've designed that and it's ready to put up."

"So you're an artist as well as a craftsman."

"I've never really known the difference. A fine craftsman is certainly an artist. But," he adds with a ghost of a smile, "I don't know if a poor artist can ever be called a craftsman. It's a thin line between the two, once you're doing carvings and things like that. I've done a number of fish, some rosewood sharks, teak sharks, boats."

"Where are these pieces?"

"Some are all over the place, a number in Toronto. And I've done nudes and mermaids and things like that out of teak. My own designs. It's not really that far from doing—deciding—a half-model. Relatively simple to do." I seem to hear David's voice. "It's all in the proportions. And the coordination. What you have to do—and you can only do it when you're reasonably young—is to learn to use your hands, and your fingers. I see someone pick up a tool and I can tell what he can do with it. Young fellows come into my shop, they don't have to tell me what they can do—I take them over to the bench and give them a piece of wood and say, now here, go at it."

And I see David walking, in the silent film clips, from bench to hull, from bench to hull to saw.

"I can tell from their movements how well they're coordinated—not just with their hands but with their feet—and how they approach something. If a person has to walk around with a board for half an hour before he decides that he's going to saw it, that doesn't do anything for you."

Murray leans over the picnic table toward me, his large-fingered hands held up as if he were grasping a plank. He is more of a raconteur, potentially more of a codger, than David. "I shouldn't really say much about this, because it's not absolutely decided, but I've already started talking to some people in Halifax about a new phase. It's coming, it has to come—we have to preserve our crafts, our craftsmanship. Pass them on to the new generation. But not just the old — the modern, too, the most up-to-date technology there is. That's what we'll be looking at, developing. From the broad adz to the dubbing adz to the computer that can take a piece of wood and lay it out ready for the saw — or perhaps cut it with lasers. Cut with lasers and ready to apply to the boat itself. The old methods known and understood and preserved — *and* the new. Just very exciting."

The sun has entered the treetops behind the yacht club. Florence and the younger generation — young David, Margaret Anne and Mora — who have been waiting patiently at another picnic table across the lawn, pick up their bags and carryalls and start slowly across toward us.

"Well, if you want to get philosophical, you can say that what we're really here for is to pass something on to the next generation. Or try to. To try to teach the followers what has been done. I certainly worked around and observed my father for many years — and all the different boats, the half-models that he did. Some that my grandfather did. I don't remember my great-grandfather, but I've seen his models — his half-models, *my great-grandfather's half-models*, one of which I have at home, and very proud of that. Yes," he looks up at the family waiting for him, holding sweaters and bags, "it's about a hundred years. A hundred years now — and maybe it'll go on for that again."

Driving north out of Lunenburg the next morning, through the abrupt little hills with square farmhouses perched on their tops, I think about the next generation, and think that David is bringing his grandchildren along very slowly on the *Kathi Anne*. After ten years, they are still before the mast, working the foredecks, with only an occasional moment granted at the helm during a race.

Then I remember that yesterday, sitting in the broken-backed chairs of the yacht club's lounge, David had talked about this.

"Robbie and Michael were in the shop with me the other

night. I told them, I said, now listen boys—when I started sailing with my dad, I *never* got the wheel. And I took mental notes of the way Dad trimmed the sails, the way he steered—everything that was going on. And after ten summers with him I could step back and take the wheel and take over. So you're getting the best experience these summers now that you could possibly get."

He had paused, then said matter-of-factly, "And of course, regardless of anything, I haven't got too many years to do it."

David is spare with praise, but he looked across the club-room to where the grandchildren were sitting at a table near the front windows, and paid them the compliment that means the most on Second Peninsula.

"If I had to sail around the world, that's the crew I'd want."

# EPILOGUE:
## JANUARY 1989

*T*he hull of the *Dorothy*, a forty-foot schooner, looks enormous in the boatshop. The deckhouse is just below the roof stringers, so you'd have to kneel on deck to work on it. An open jar of white lead and a putty knife lie on the scaffolding where David had been caulking the deck seams. On the afterdeck an old black-and-red plaid shirt, the kind I have seen in so many photographs and film clips of David, lies crumpled up like a rag.

It is the day after David Stevens' funeral, which took place on a Wednesday afternoon in January, in a small, pentecostal church in the town of Mahone Bay, and I have come out to stand in the boatshop in near-zero weather and look at David Stevens' last boat.

Yesterday five hundred people crammed the sanctuary of the Calvary Temple with its plain walls and plain gothic windows, and spilled over into the vestibule and into the Sunday school building that adjoins the side of the church. Nearly a third of the pews in the sanctuary were reserved for the Stevens families, many of them elderly, proud and erect in their black suits and black dresses. The program of the service had a photograph of the *Kathi Anne* under sail on the cover and the words from Hebrews, 12:1, on which the minister based his eulogy, "And let us run with patience the race that is set before us."

David Peill told me the story, which is typical David Stevens, that the previous Sunday morning this eighty-one-year-old had gone to the barn and hauled down fifteen bales of hay for his cows, then decided he wasn't feeling too well and went in the house to sit down for a bit. Evelyn knew to phone a neighboring couple, both doctors. David was removing his shirt for the examination when he collapsed and died. I think we were all astounded at the news. We thought he would go on forever.

On the way down the peninsula this morning I stopped at the grave site where David's body was interred yesterday. The Second Peninsula Cemetery has no sign. I parked on the shoulder of the road, walked around a wrought-iron gate and down a pebble pathway through locust and pine trees. Twenty yards ahead there is a clearing in the woods with grass that is surprisingly green for a deep January morning. Beyond the clearing the trees thin out and sunlight glints off the ice on Martin Cove.

Yesterday had been grey and bleak, with just a moment of sunlight at the end of the burial service, like an amen. Today the scene is frozen but sunny. I look at the other names that are as familiar to me now as if I'd met them — Berringer, Rhodenizer, Backman — and then at the Stevens plots — two brothers, Amos and Cecil, and the man who earned the title of patriarch, Randolph B. Stevens, 1881–1965. I envy them and David this beautiful place.

It was my intention to call briefly at the house, just out of courtesy, not to bother Evelyn after a long and draining day yesterday. But Dorothy is there and Evelyn is bright as a bird, and we end up spending several hours reminiscing with gusto about him. Evelyn is in a wheelchair; her leg was amputated at the knee last year, and though she wears a prosthesis, she wheels herself vigorously about the house because she can move faster that way. She wheels into the living room and is up, walking along holding onto the bookcases, pulling out photo albums. We look through some and talk about the times shown there. There is a set of pictures of David constructing a hull, step by careful step. There are pictures of the schooner races at La Have in '84, and we find ourselves talking about events that I've written about, that have become family lore, and I have this strange feeling about a book, which comes out of life, circling back into life and becoming part of it. This is a morning for remembering, this morning after the funeral, and "writing down," as the old drunk on Tancook called it, is the servant of remembering.

I've spent twenty minutes walking around the hull of the *Dorothy* or just standing, looking at her, while my feet grow progressively more numb and a black and white cat who inhabits the boatshop watches me. This is a magical place and I don't want to leave. I notice a front window where the same missing pane is still patched with a piece of rough plank, the bark along one edge. The *Dorothy* looks huge, huge in the middle of the boatshop. She looms up like a whale I once saw suspended overhead in a science museum, and I stand there with frozen feet marveling one more time at what a man eighty-one years old can create—alone.

David's boats will last for generations, the skills that built them for more than that. There were many epitaphs spoken for David yesterday, and many more will be said privately by the thousands who knew him, but one is special. Evelyn's benediction has a humor that could almost be David's. "If there's a piece of wood up there, he'll find it."

*Schooner Master* was designed by Ann Aspell.
It was typeset in Sabon by
Dartmouth Printing Company.
It was printed on Rivertone, an acid-free
paper, by The Book Press, Inc.

TOO SIMPLE TO FAIL